Activatin...

1001

Academic Words for IELTS

...and other English language tests

By Keith Burgess

Adams & Austen Press - Sydney, Australia

About the Author

Keith Burgess has been working at the chalk face of EAP (English for Academic Purposes) since 1992. Of particular interest to him has been the question of how to move Intermediate, and especially Upper Intermediate, students closer to the status of first language users.

Keith has a degree in linguistics from Canterbury University and a TESOL qualification.

Acknowledgements

The author would like to thank the following people for their help in reviewing and/or trialling the materials used in this book:

Canterbury Language College (Australasia), for providing facilities, students and the freedom to develop the resource over a number of years, and especially to Wang Xiao Xuan and David Pepperle. I am grateful also to the hundreds of students who participated in the development of this resource and especially Ok Hee Lee, Coco k.k. Liang, Valentina Shevchenko and Kato Hirata.

Also thanks to the students of Aspect International Language Academy for insisting on 1001 and not 101 academic words. Thanks also to Terry Peck for taking on such a huge publishing project, prompting the revision extension, pronunciation and spelling exercises, and putting together the Crosswords, Hangman and Wordfind games.

Interactive Online IELTS Course

101 Helpful Hints Interactive Online Course for IELTS

http://ielts101.aapress.com.au

Published by Adams & Austen Press

101 Helpful Hints for IELTS - Academic Module - International Edition:

Book: *ISBN 978-0-9587604-6-1*
Cassette: *ISBN 978-0-9578980-0-4**
Bk+Audio CD: *ISBN 978-0-9578980-6-6*

101 Helpful Hints for IELTS - General Training Module - International Edition:

Book: *ISBN 978-0-9587604-9-2*
Cassette: *ISBN 978-0-9578980-0-4**
Bk+Audio CD: *ISBN 978-0-9578980-9-7*

202 Useful Exercises for IELTS - International Edition

Book: *ISBN 978-0-9587604-7-8*
Cassette: *ISBN 978-0-9578980-1-1*
Bk+ CDs(2): *ISBN 978-0-9578980-7-3*

202 Useful Exercises for IELTS - Australasian Edition

Book: *ISBN 978-0-9587604-5-4*
Cassette: *ISBN 978-0-9578980-2-8*
Bk+ CDs(2): *ISBN 978-0-9578980-5-9*

404 Essential Tests for IELTS - Academic Module - International Edition:

Book: *ISBN 978-0-9751832-0-5*
Cassettes(2): *ISBN 978-0-9751832-1-2**
Bk+ CDs(2): *ISBN 978-0-9751832-2-9*
Study Guide: *ISBN 978-0-9751832-8-1***

404 Essential Tests for IELTS - General Training Module - International Edition:

Book: *ISBN 978-0-9751832-3-6*
Cassettes(2): *ISBN 978-0-9751832-1-2**
Bk & CDs(2): *ISBN 978-0-9751832-4-3*
Study Guide: *ISBN 978-0-9751832-9-8***

* *the listening test is the same for both Modules of the test*

** *Multimedia CD-ROM - video, audio and practice tests*

Published in Sydney, Australia 2007

ISBN 978-0-9578980-3-5

Adams & Austen Press Pty. Ltd. A.B.N. 96 087 873 943
PO Box 509, Marrickville, New South Wales, Australia 1475
Tel: 612-9590-4469 Fax: 612-9590-4471
Email: *aap@aapress.com.au* *www.aapress.com.au*

Foreword

One fundamental requirement for a good score in IELTS – or any other complex English language test – is the possession of a well-developed vocabulary. This is not at all surprising; teachers and students alike instinctively know when it is the lack of words that is holding back progress.

First and foremost, a chosen word must be right for its purpose. Finding the right word or phrase can be frustrating at times for native English speakers, but English language learners are disadvantaged by being unable to hear if their choice is appropriate. Something else must suffice and that can really only be targeted practice. Secondly, if its acquisition is to be of any real value, a new word or phrase must be familiar within a variety of contexts.

Keith's Method achieves both aims; that of acquisition and correct application. With regular study a student's word bank will quickly enlarge, and the vocabulary will belong where it is used – all in the shortest amount of time.

The Method is in three parts; it is simple to apply, and it works. Try it and see.

Terry Peck

How the 1001 Superwords and phrases were selected:

“ These 1001 words and phrases were culled from various freely available word lists of universities and texts. Words that were thought to be too commonplace such as "transport", "adult" or "odd" were rejected, as were words that seemed too specific to academic subjects such as "aggregate", "chapter" and "ethic".

If the Academic Word List of The School of Linguistics and Applied Language Studies of Victoria University, Wellington, is consulted, it will be found that 345 of the first 500 headwords are included. Not only the so-called headwords were used, but there has been a conscious effort to present a variety of forms. These words were also found to have high frequency in academic texts. ”

Keith Burgess

CONTENTS

CONTENTS continued...

Pages

Spoken Word Puzzles continued...

for students...

Principles of "Activating 1001 Academic Words for IELTS"

The course is designed to teach you quickly and easily the language you need for success in IELTS and similar examinations and at university level study.

What this resource does for you

- Makes vocabulary learning simple through a three-part process. Learning academic language does not have to be difficult or time-consuming.
- Invites you to understand the meaning and use of words by looking at an easy context. English can be learned in the same way that you came to know your own first language.
- Teaches you to observe and analyse language easily. No grammar rules to learn. You can use the knowledge you have gathered right away!
- Gives you the opportunity to "think" in English and develop this necessary skill for communicating at university level.
- Allows you to experience the word (its meaning and use) at least six times to deepen your understanding and ability to use the word.
- Makes it possible for you to learn within a short time (not years but weeks) the 1001 words and phrases you absolutely need to be able to use.
- Steadily builds your knowledge, ability and confidence to use the words. First, you comprehend the basic meaning; then you see and practise using the words and phrases in wider contexts.

How this resource works

This resource:

- Informs you how to analyse vocabulary for use.
- Presents a sentence with words and a context that are easily understood.
- Offers a half sentence to be completed that tests your understanding of meaning and use.
- Invites you to construct your own sentence from your own ideas or imagined context.
- Activates your memory and ability to use the language through paraphrasing; that is, giving you sentences to write using the words.
- Gives you a chance to "think through" the language by answering a "word puzzle" by yourself or in conversation with others.
- Provides the opportunity to improve your knowledge and expertise through spelling, pronunciation, revision and extension exercises.

The Method

Every teacher has been frustrated, but not dismayed, at the disparity between the *passive* knowledge of their students and their *active* use of it. I think every teacher has walked out of a classroom at the end of a lesson feeling pleased that their students have seemingly absorbed the targeted language and exercised control of it, and then suddenly been disappointed to overhear the same students, not only immediately omit the language from expression outside of class, but also operate at a level far below their assigned level. Students studying at an Intermediate level are overheard to be performing at an Elementary level, and perhaps even struggle to put subject+verb (+object) English sentences together.

I am certain that every teacher acknowledges, too, the sheer difficulty of putting all the pieces of a second language together. We are – or should not really be – surprised, for example, that despite being taught a variety of academic language terms, many students rely on a relatively small and constant range of language. A genuine Upper Intermediate student would identify the verbs *"see"*, *"observe"* and *"witness"* as having similarities in meaning, but use *"see"* as a blanket verb. Likewise, this student would use Past Simple reliably and accurately in recounting a story, but would typically not combine in a single utterance a combination of tense or aspect or add another structural complication. *("I've never met a local who works more than forty hours a week.")* Teachers will say that it takes time and multiple exposures.

Yet teachers (and language schools) do not always acknowledge that many or most courses are regarded as intensive by the student. The student has allowed him or herself six months study to gain confidence for living, or the bare minimum to continue the expensive business of getting an education. Our reaction as teachers is to say we are providing *"a dip in the ocean"* or *"we are planting the seed (for later fruition)"* and the student is just being *"too ambitious and unrealistic"*.

At the higher levels we tend to teach ever more exotic structures (*"What I realised was"*, *"It's time I was gone"* – as the course books dictate) or specialist vocabulary around more and more cerebral topics. Or we rely on fluency practice as a means of getting students to a point when they might use *"witness"* over *"see"*. Or we trust that by immersion, they will experience the language in a variety of contexts.

The truth of the matter is that fluency practice can be a bland (albeit good for boosting confidence and oiling the wheels) or highly functional context (*"this is the language for making offers"*), and the student will not ever voluntarily or spontaneously use the word until required to respond with it. *("Everyone can see the unfair treatment of females in your country especially in the workplace!", "Well, I've never witnessed it myself!")*.

Every teacher has been astounded and pleased, too, at observing the improvements in fluency that students gain from living the language. Students sooner or later leave the classroom to function in the real world, and, when they do, the interaction experienced reinforces the knowledge gained in the classroom, and the ongoing to and fro of regular communication in a second language makes language use a habit and gives users confidence.

However, when these same students are assessed before entering an English college again, it is often found that it is only their speaking and listening skills at a social level that have improved; there has been only an incremental increase in new language – or it is highly colloquial. The assessor and teacher note significant gaps in the knowledge, and there is not a great depth to the conversational skills. When pressed to fully explain or provide details or counter argue in a debate, silence and hesitation replace the former flow of words.

This situation may be alright for English second language users who wish to operate with the language in a highly functional way in the workplace; for example, to work on the shop floor, or for a person who has the opportunity to resort to the first language for intimate communication. But teachers involved in EAP programmes are, of course, concerned most about their students ultimately failing at tertiary level – due not to their ability or motivation, but solely to their expertise in English. So here is the problem.

Obviously, students cannot fully experience their English for years in a classroom. The classroom imparts knowledge and allows practice, but in the real world of interaction the genuine learning occurs. However, the level plateaus, or the accumulation of further knowledge and the prompting of active use halts or is gradual unless the student has special gifts or is a great reader. What is the solution? The solution is a truly intensive programme.

Firstly, the student needs to be equipped with a bare knowledge of a wide range of language so that this knowledge can be reinforced in the wider environment now and later. Thus, the student also needs multiple accessible but brief contexts in order to get a quick but deep initiation to the word or structure; a chance, in essence, to have *"thought through the word"*. The student needs to revisit the word, have an opportunity to retrieve it time and again, and to have confirmed his or her own understanding of it, and to articulate the word or to react to it; that is, to experience the language as the first language acquirer who experiences multiple exposures and challenges to react.

Secondly, it would benefit the student immensely to become a natural observer of language. This entails not only the ability to absorb meaning from context, but also be aware of the function of the word and the way in which the word fits into a sentence. As explained below, this amounts to observing what precedes and follows the word in the model sentence(s) or the *"pattern of the word"*. In my experience, this may start out as a determinedly conscious effort for the students, but sooner or later becomes an effortless and subconscious skill.

In this resource these multiple exposures take the form of:

STEP 1. Read the Superword or phrase. Note its pronunciation. Practice saying it.

STEP 2. Read the model sentence. Read it again. Make sure you understand the meaning of the Superword within the context of the model. Try this without the use a dictionary...

21 **account for** /əˈkaʊnt fɔː/

" The fact that people are unable to see the daily misery that people experience in third world countries **accounts for** so much of the world's wealth remaining in the hands of so few people. "

STEP 3. Look at Questions 1 and 2. Try to complete the spaces in the sentences with reference to the Superword.

Q1. The fact that Most women in Africa still [illegible] ....

accounts for the majority of top politicians still being male.

Q2. The fact that foreign students find it difficult to study subjects at university in which there is a heavy English content ***accounts for***...

Their incompetence in English ....

STEP 4. If this is difficult (if you think you can't do it), read the model sentence again carefully, and try again.

STEP 5. Check your answer with the suggested answer.

STEP 6. If you still cannot do it, do this: analyse the word this way.

a. What is the meaning of the word? Use other words to give the meaning.

b. What kind of word is it? (A noun?...or a verb?...or an adjective? etc.)

c. How do you use the word?

i. What is the word's pattern? What words go before it and what words go after it?

ii. Are there any words that conveniently go with this word?

iii. Now try to answer the question again.

STEP 7. Make a new sentence using the word:

Q3. One more:
....
....

The student is given an opportunity to absorb meaning and use with a slowed down and repeated and simplified exposure to it. Through this process the language sensitivity of the student is fully exploited, and studying language does not become a subject akin to mathematics, but an experience close to the first language user's experience.

Although the emphasis is on "experience", the student should be encouraged to become an automatic analyser of language and practise this initially a lot before relying solely on comprehension of the model sentence. Analysis entails being aware of basic meaning, what kind of word it is (noun, verb etc.), but also – importantly – what goes *before* the word and what (if anything) comes *after* (the "pattern" of the word), as well as the noting of collocations.

____________________ **account(s) for** ____________________

BEFORE **AFTER**

Examples of various patterns are:

VERBS

something **accounts for** *something*
somebody **accounts** to *somebody* **for** *something*

NOUNS

an account of *something*

Here are some examples of **collocations** – students are told that these are words that can go often and comfortably with the word they are studying:

VERBS

account(s) for *a situation* / *the behaviour* / *the matter* / (*a problem*)
that **accounts for** *it*
unable to **account for** (*something*)

NOUNS

a true **account** *a satisfactory* **account**

Along with multiple exposures, a student needs to confirm an understanding of and ability to use the word – and this can be easily achieved via *paraphrase*.

PARAPHRASING SENTENCES

Instructions: **Now review vocabulary items 1 – 40 so that you are well prepared to complete the following exercises which ask you to "think through" the language a little more.**

Rewrite these sentences using the words in brackets.

(Note: sometimes you have to change the sentences a lot, and you might not always need the article or preposition.)

21. The fact that so many more tourists are coming to New Zealand can be explained by the fact that other parts of the world seem so dangerous to visit now. ***(account for)***

    ....

Students need to go beyond passive understanding and need to be challenged to think through the language, too, or to react to the word originally. This can be achieved as a first step through *Word Puzzles* solved with a partner:

WORD PUZZLES

Instructions: **Think through the vocabulary and increase your speaking skills by taking turns at asking and answering these questions.**

Try to use the lesson words as you answer:

21. What **accounts for** it? The streets are wet but it hasn't been raining.

Students are encourage to extend and revise through a number of playful exercises too. For example; students can be persuaded to become aware of differences in meaning and recognize *formal* versus *informal* contexts:

A. Match the **verbs** with their **synonyms**:

intend **substitute** **discard** **plan** **swap** **throw away**

B. Use the Lesson words and synonyms above to complete these sentences. Choose the best one for each pair.

a. I was never able to claim the Lotto prize because I .... the ticket by mistake and of course I cannot remember its number.

b. Packaging is not a waste if it is kept as part of a gift, but if people .... the packaging it creates a problem of rubbish disposal.

HINT *'discard' means 'throw away' because you have decided that you don't want it.*

And students can practise changing *form* and *function*:

A. Make these **adjectives** into **adverbs**.

deceptive **enthusiastic** **significant**

B. Now join the **adverbs** to the **adjectives** or **–ed verb forms** in these sentences and take out the unnecessary language.

a. The instructions for using the machine seemed simple, but actually they were very hard to follow.

CLUE *The instructions for using the machine are deceptively simple.*

b. If a teacher has a strong sense of humour, he or she will be listened to with a great deal of attention and delight the students.

c. The highways in and out of the city are much busier at rush hour and this has a huge effect.

Becoming further aware of *collocations* may enhance the students' sensitivity to language too:

A. Match these **adjectives** with the **nouns** they can go with:

sufficient **curious** **hazardous** **sustainable** **apparent**

phenomenon **waste** **development** **energy** **failure**

B. Use the combinations of **adjectives** and **nouns** above to make simple sentences about each of these situations:

a. The chemicals from the process can harm humans.

b. There is more than enough electricity to supply all the households.

c. Building fifteen new factories each year will not harm the environment very much.

d. The advertisement asking the public for money for a new hospital has brought no money so far.

e. Although fewer people say they believe in god, more people are attending church.

HINT *Answer to a:* *'The waste is hazardous.'*

Students can practise getting words out for situations (*natural elicitation*):

A. Make sure you have REVISED ALL THE LANGUAGE FOR THIS SECTION.

Study the situation below carefully and choose one word or phrase from the forty you have examined in the lesson that can best be applied to it:

> " This society is very unlike my own. Here prostitution is legal. Young people are allowed to drink in public bars at only seventeen. It is also legal to smoke marijuana in public bars, such as in cafés. "

Did you choose the same word or phrase as an English first language user?

B. Make a simple sentence using this word.

Beyond The Method

There is a myriad of other games and activities that students can be enticed to play to reinforce their accumulated knowledge of lexis. At the same time as the 1001 academic words are worked at in the Method, a structural review can take place with the same principal of asking the student to think through the language and to dexterously and originally manipulate it. A variety of structures including passives, tenses, complex subjects and objects and conditionals should be taught productively. Complementary study should demand an active use of the language in the same way that this resource does.

The typical English learner may not be a great lover of English or of learning languages. In addition to acknowledging a student's limitations and other aspirations besides learning English, we ought to give credit to the various qualities that many students wish to bring to their study of English. For example, students' awareness of new language does not often result in immediate memorisation of it, but they are prepared to wait and look out for it and experience it again.

Most importantly, we can give credit to the sensitivity and linguistic intuition our students show towards the language and, in the classroom, try to duplicate the first language user's experience. Finally, we ought also to acknowledge the extraordinary work ethic of the many students who come from cultures which prize education and knowledge.

The intensive teaching programme above (of which this Method can be a part) represents an intellectual challenge which students rise up to and makes the classroom experience a highly productive and exciting one.

An additional in-depth guide to the Method can be accessed online at:

http://aapress.com.au/1001/theMethod.html

How to use this resource

In this vocabulary learning method there are twenty-five (25) lessons to study, each with forty (40) academic words and phrases to learn – plus one demonstration word.

A total of 1001 Superwords and phrases.

The method is divided into three parts:

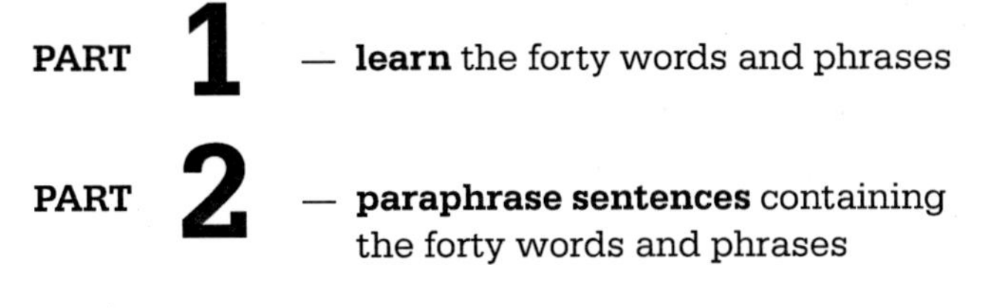

PART 1 — **learn** the forty words and phrases

PART 2 — **paraphrase sentences** containing the forty words and phrases

PART 3 — **speak** the forty words and phrases in sentences with a partner

In addition, there are revision, spelling and pronunciation exercises for every lesson.

****

IT IS NOT ESSENTIAL TO PRACTISE WITH THE OPTIONAL EXERCISES

(There are 1001 words to learn – the optional exercises are for further practice only.)

****

Before you begin,
TEST YOURSELF to discover your current academic word skill ability and level...

Academic Word Test – Structure

TEST YOURSELF

INSTRUCTIONS:

Before you use the 1001 Academic Word resource, find a quiet place and take your time to complete each of the test sections above to the best of your ability.

Check your score with the Scoring System on page xiii.

The Academic Word Test can also be found on the CD...

A shorter version of the test can also be taken.

Short Test: Sections 1 to 9 only. (100 points)
Full Test: Sections 1 to 10. (160 points)

(Section 10 is self-scored.)

TEST ANSWERS ON PAGE 129 OF THE BOOK

1 ACADEMIC WORD RECOGNITION

A Choose a word or phrase from the box below which has a similar meaning to each of the words **a–k**: **11 points**

a great deal	excitement	warn	deteriorate
shorten	timetable	plan	improve
whole	become aware		courageous

a. alert ....
b. substantial ....
c. worsen ....
d. realise ....
e. fearless ....
f. scheme ....
g. schedule ....
h. abbreviate ....
i. enhance ....
j. exhilaration ....
k. entire ....

B Do the same for words **l–v**: **11 points**

environment	at first	own	let down
event	collect	popularity	share
unbroken	build	vow	

l. gather ....
m. possess ....
n. pledge ....
o. construct ....
p. atmosphere ....
q. disappoint ....
r. occasion ....
s. apportion ....
t. intact ....
u. initially ....
v. fame ....

2 RECOGNITION OF MEANING, FORM AND FUNCTION

Use these words to complete the sentences below: **5 points**

inform **precisely** **advocate** **correct** **eventually**

a. The volcano erupted at .... six thirty-four in the morning.

b. It is not unusual for people to .... capital punishment if a member of their own family has been murdered.

c. If you are travelling overseas, you should .... members of your family about where you are going and what time you will be there for your safety.

d. I believe that .... all countries will be democratic, although it may take a hundred years.

e. I don't always trust the news that I hear on television. Often the facts or the details are not ....

3 RECOGNITION OF DIFFERENCES IN MEANING.

A Match the **academic** words a–d with the **everyday** words of similar meaning below: **4 points**

find **start** **bring/take** **count**

a. discover ....
b. calculate ....
c. deliver ....
d. initiate ....

B Now choose the **best answer** from the same pairs of words in **3A** to complete the following sentences: **8 points**

a. (i) For years I have been trying to .... the right person to marry.

(ii) There has been a lot of research but nobody .... a definite cure for diabetes.

b. (i) The government has failed to .... improvements in health care that it promised.

(ii) The new health care system .... a great many problems to medical staff.

c. (i) Either partner in a marriage (the husband or the wife) can .... a divorce.

(ii) It can be either the husband or the wife who .... the arguments that lead to divorce.

d. (i) I put all my spare money into a jar and after three months I take it out and .... it.

(ii) I want to get a car and pay it off each month. But first I will have to .... how much it will cost me each week.

4 CHANGING FORM

A Change these **verbs** into **nouns** using the suffixes below: **6 points**

-cation **-ion** **-ment** **-ation** **-ing**

a. preserve ....
b. select ....

d. compensate ....
e. resent ....
f. upgrade ....

B Now rewrite the first part of the sentences below choosing the **noun** to fit the descriptions **a–f**: **6 points**

a. To make sure you have the right candidate is important for a political party.

....

b. To keep the historical documents in good condition is important.

....

c. To put high walls and weapons around the city is overdue.

....

d. To make the public transport more modern from time to time is necessary.

....

e. Feeling hate for and being jealous of siblings is common.

....

f. It took thousands of labourers hundreds of years to construct the Pyramids.

....

C Change these **adjectives** into **adverbs**: **6 points**

a. microscopic ....
b. modest ....
c. ideal ....
d. drastic ....
e. genuine ....
f. immature ....

D Rewrite these sentences using the **adverb** forms above: **6 points**

a. He behaves very young for his age.

....

b. The house is situated in exactly the right place.

....

c. The government has changed the taxation laws far too much.

....

d. Some people don't believe he is sorry, but I do. I think he really means it.

....

e. Despite their high qualifications, the computer programmers were paid quite little.

....

f. The paintings were impressive because they were drawn with incredible detail.

....

5 RECOGNITION OF COLLOCATIONS

A Match the **adjectives a–d** with the things they can describe: *(Use all of the things listed in the box.)* **8 points**

school	progress	damage	resources
harm	gift	restaurant	supply

a. extraordinary ....
b. exclusive ....
c. irreparable ....
d. abundant ....

B Make simple sentences using the combinations above: **4 points**

Begin: **"It was… "**

a. Only the wealthy were able to afford to eat there.

....

b. There was enough oil stockpiled to last ten years.

....

c. In five years the nation went from being the fifth poorest to the third wealthiest in the world.

....

d. The son could never forget the physical punishment the father had given him. It destroyed their relationship.

....

6 TESTING RANGE I

A Which word can you use to replace the underlined words? **4 points**

historical **ephemeral** **available** **complex**

a. Life is very short.

....

b. University education should be there for everyone to have.

....

c. Young people like to get married in very old buildings.

....

d. Statistics can be hard to understand.

....

B Match the correct word and add it to sentences **a–d**: **4 points**

Admittedly **Surprisingly** **Historically** **Typically**

a. .... , people who are newly retired become depressed in the first months of retirement.

b. ...., humans have caused some animals to become extinct, but they have saved many creatures too.

c. ...., the church in this country has played an important part in government.

d. ...., McDonalds food is very nutritious despite some of the food being fried.

C In which of the following sentences do you want to use... **3 points**

the extent of, **as well as** or **as is the case with** ?

a. It is a good idea to take essential medicines with you when you go on a hike .... bandages, since you might have an accident.

b. The storm seems to have destoyed the whole city. They are worried about .... the damage and loss of life.

c. Because people can now go online to get the most up-to-date information, interest in newspapers is declining .... magazines and encyclopaedias.

7 TESTING RANGE II

Rewrite the underlined parts of the sentences using: **4 points**

locally **regionally** **nationally** **globally**

a. The parliament is in control of the country.

....

b. The City Council is in control in this city.

....

c. No country or body is in control of the world.

....

d. The Provincial Government is in control beyond the city and through the countryside.

....

8 TESTING RANGE III

A Complete these sentences: **3 points**

a. Women are commonly employed today as hairdressers, receptionists and accounts clerks. Unfortunately, **such** .... has relatively low status and pay.

b. Modern cities have comfortable and efficient buses and underground trains. **Such** .... allows the people to move around easily without seriously polluting the atmosphere.

c. Although 50% of plastic containers are reusable, half of them are sent to landfill instead of being used again. **Such** .... makes products 10% more expensive than they should be.

B Which of the sentence endings **a–d** can complete the sentence below? Choose one and circle it. **1 point**

During the Second World, I lived with my brothers and sisters and mother in the countryside. **Meanwhile**, ...

a. ...my cousins lived in the city of London where the bombs fell every day.

b. ...nowadays, I live in the city alone.

c. ...other children lived in the countryside too.

d. ...war separates a lot of families and causes a great deal of heartache.

9 KNOWING HOW WORDS ARE PUT TOGETHER

A **dis – proportion – ate – ly** **4 points**

a. What is the **stem noun**? ....

b. Make the **noun** an **adjective**: ....

c. Make the **adjective negative**: ....

d. Make the **adjective** a **negative adverb**:

....

B The numbers below are statistics for the country of Caludonis. Complete a simple sentence for each set of statistics using **disproportionately high** or **disproportionately low**. Use each phrase once only. **2 points**

a. Total number of female workers – 100,000
Part-time female workers – 23,000
Total number of male workers – 200,000
Part-time male workers – 54,000

The number of part-time male workers is ....

....

b. The number of child deaths – 35
The total number of deaths – 275,000
The child death rate in other countries is 1,000 for every 500,000 people.

The number of child deaths is ....

....

10 THINKING THROUGH ACADEMIC LANGUAGE

A **Paraphrasing**. Write these sentences again using the vocabulary in brackets:

a. I thought the cost of the trip would be a lot less than it actually was. ***(underestimate)*** **4 points**

....

b. Apparently, tonnes of dust from outer space lands on the Earth each year. ***(deposit)*** **4 points**

....

c. Nobody lived in the area for years, because the land was too expensive to buy. ***(vacant)*** **4 points**

....

B Complete these sentences logically:

a. **With the exception of** the planet Earth, ...
.... in this solar system seem to be without life. **4 points**

b. Fourteen year old boys are too young to drink alcohol. **Likewise,** .... **4 points**

c. It is a little bit of an unusual school. The students study self-defense and communication skills **along with**
.... **4 points**

d. Grapes have been in short supply to the wine making industry this year; **hence,** .... **4 points**

e. The Minki whale population is reported to be quite large in sub-Antarctic waters. **Elsewhere,** ....
.... **4 points**

f. Good staff leave for better opportunities and rewards. He gives his staff six weeks holiday a year; **thereby,** ...
.... **4 points**

C Answer these questions as fully as you can using the given word or phrase:

a. Can you explain why religion and going to church are so much less popular these days? ***(account for)*** **4 points**

....

....

b. If a basketball player hits another player in a game, say, punches him in the face, what do you think is the right punishment? ***(justify)*** **4 points**

....

....

c. Why do couples choose to have such small families these days (i.e. with only one or two children)? ***(be largely due to)*** **4 points**

....

....

d. The parents could buy a house (which they have always wanted, but never had), but instead they use the money to provide their child with a good education. What does it **testify** to? **4 points**

....

....

e. The couple both had very high paying jobs, but their children needed looking after when neither was at home and their employers expected them to entertain clients at home. So, what **eroded** their income? [4] **4 points**

childcare ....

....

f. What can ambulance drivers **legally** do when they are hurrying to an accident? [2] **4 points**

speed ....

....

SCORING SYSTEM:

- Award 1 point for every correct answer for Sections 1 to 9.
- For Section 10 award up to 4 points for each of your answers.
- Divide the total by 16 and multiply by 10 to obtain your percentage score.

0 – 20: You have just entered academic study. Use this resource slowly but regularly to begin to build your understanding of a wider range of vocabulary.

Aim for five words a day at first and then increase the pace. Work especially hard at understanding the whole model sentence before trying the exercises. Be tough on yourself and only look at the answers if you really need to. Although this language can seem difficult, with effort you will begin to think in English more.

Take time out to play with the language too, in the additional exercises. They are a lot of fun!

21 – 40: You have a sound basis of everyday English but a minimum knowledge of academic expression. You can use this resource to step by step expand this knowledge.

Aim for ten words a day. Take your time at first to understand the whole model sentence. Notice every word. This is important for your understanding of meaning as well as your understanding of how to use the word. Practise analysing the words as directed until you can complete the exercises with ease.

Don't forget to play with the language too, in the additional exercises. They can be fun!

41 – 60: You have knowledge of English that includes some academic vocabulary. You can use this resource to rapidly broaden, not only your knowledge, but also your active ability to write and speak with it.

We suggest you enter the resource slowly at first. Perhaps ten words a day. Take time to absorb the meaning of each model sentence well for all the 1001 words. At first analyse the words as directed until it becomes a regular habit and you can complete the exercises quite easily by studying the model only. After a while, rely on your understanding and automatic analysis of the model sentences only. This way you can quickly build your active word stock.

When you feel tired, take time out to play with the language in the revision and extension additional exercises. They are fun!

61 – 80: You already have an awareness of a good range of academic language and can apply it with some accuracy. Use this resource to add to your stock of academic vocabulary, but especially work hard at thinking through the language.

Be sure to take time to absorb the meaning of each model sentence well for all the 1001 words. At first, analyse the words as directed until it becomes a regular habit and you can complete the exercises quite easily by studying the model only. Be thoughtful about your answers. Doing this will make sure the language becomes part of your own personal lexicon – or part of the language you actively use.

Use the fun revision and extension exercises to cement your understanding and revise frequently.

81 – 100: Your awareness of language and your ability to use it is close to that of a native English speaker. Use this resource to confirm your understanding and practise your fluency.

Use your ability to understand the model sentences well before attempting the exercises. Proceed at a brisk pace. Extend yourself by thinking deeply about each sentence so that you are not only using the vocabulary correctly, but you are creating original sentences – especially when you are creating your "one more" sentence and in reply to the "word puzzles". This deeper thinking will enable the sentences to become part of your active repertoire.

The fun revision and extension exercises will enable you to recognize discreet differences in meaning and to observe collocations and other word patterns.

t h e

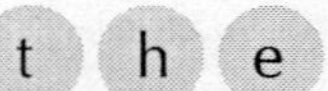

Notes

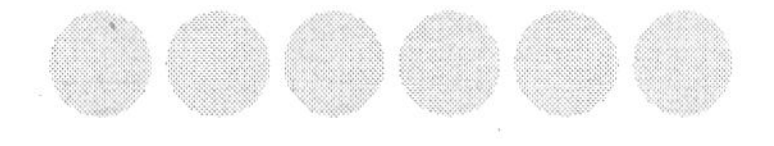

Part One is on the CD

PART ONE

...is your introduction to the 1001 SUPERWORDS AND PHRASES.

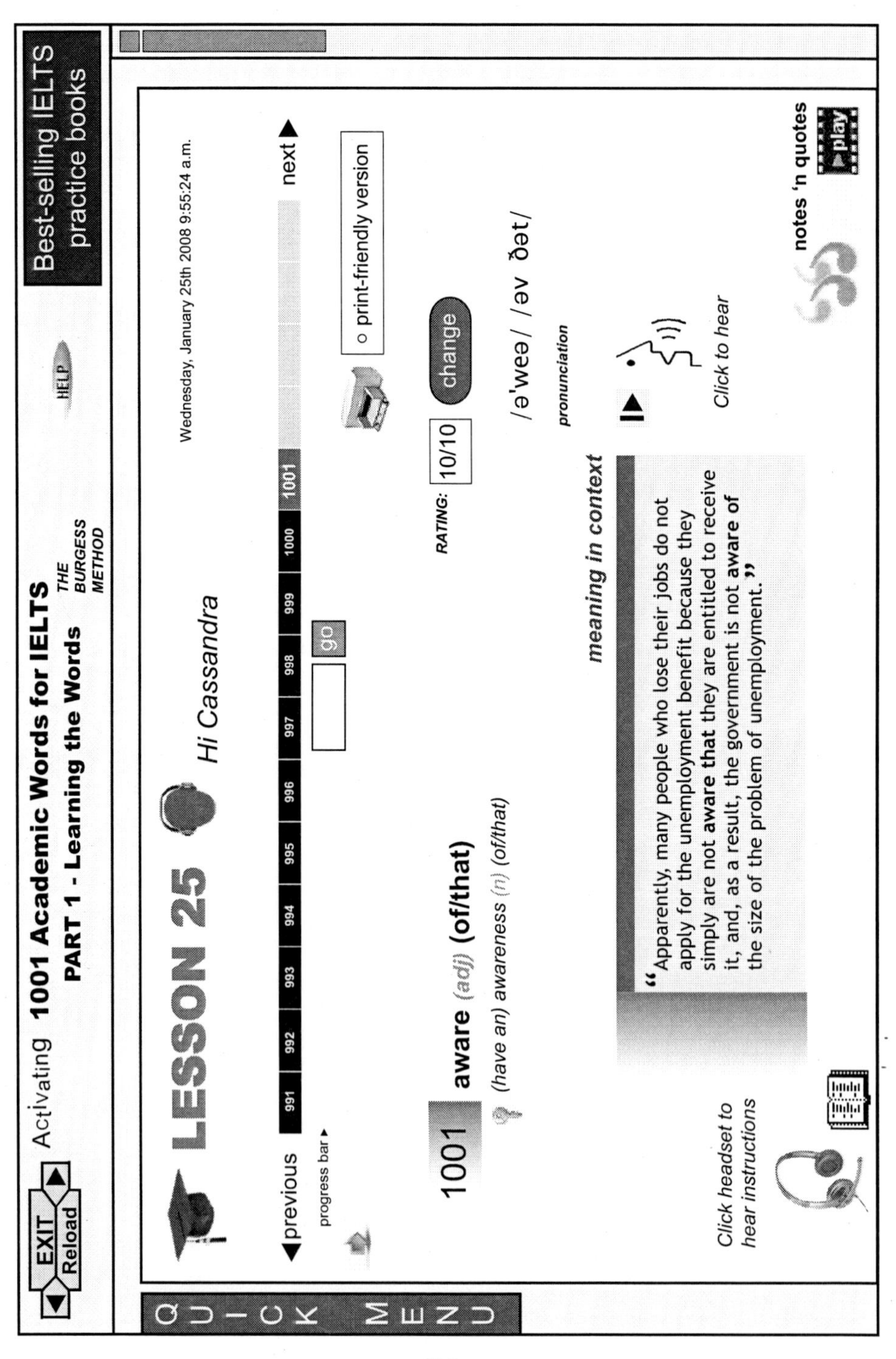

- Learn how to use the ACADEMIC WORDS in various contexts first by STUDYING THE MODEL, then COMPLETING SENTENCES to show you know the meaning. You can also RATE the words and phrases for future use.
- If you wish, you can print out the Lesson pages with the Worksheet Generator.
- Review at any time with the optional REVISION and EXTENSION exercises.

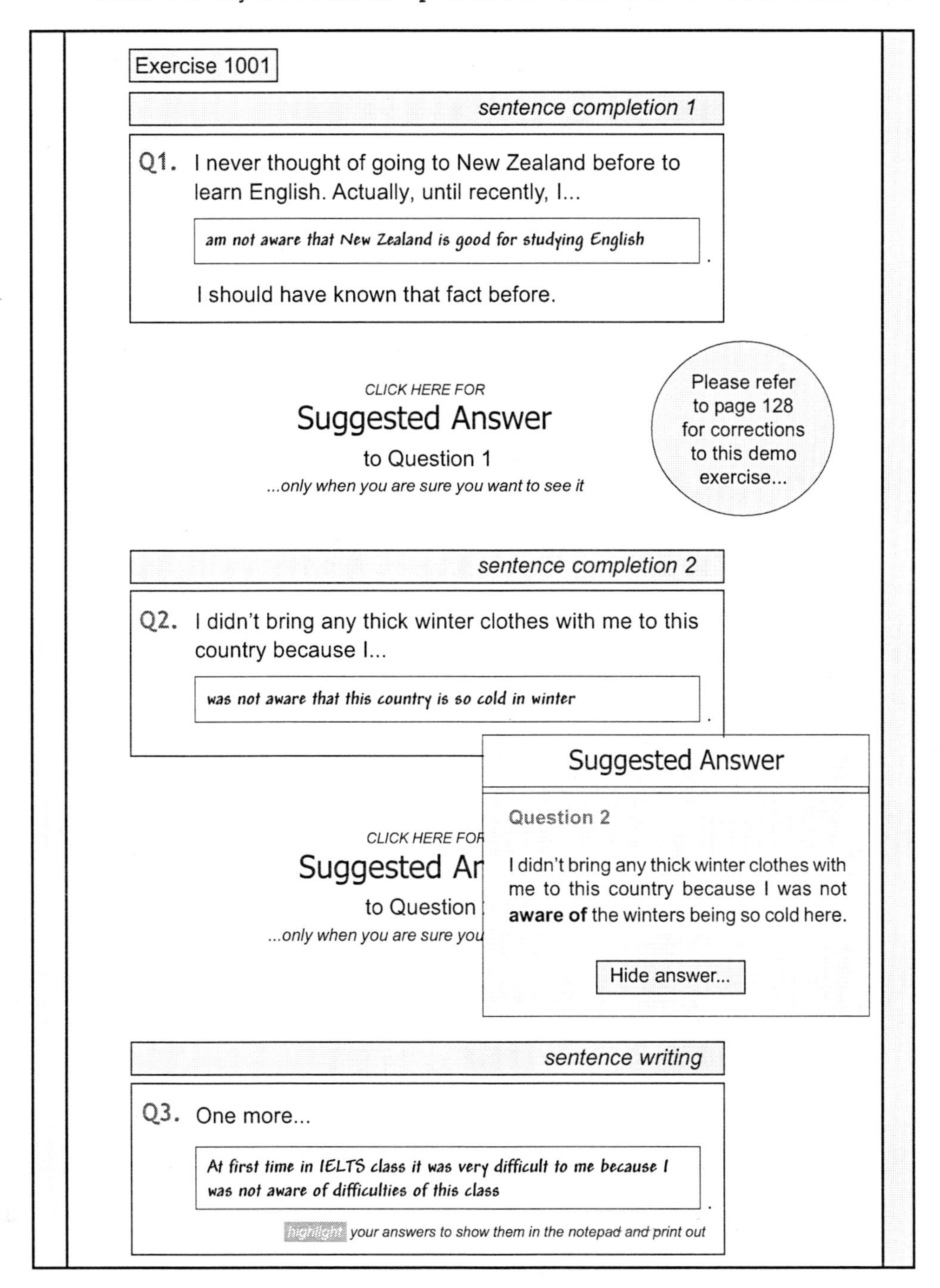

Part Two is on the CD

PART TWO

...is an extended writing exercise.

- Having studied the forty Superwords and phrases of each lesson, extend your written use of these words by PARAPHRASING GIVEN SENTENCES.
- If you wish, you can print out all the Lesson worksheets from the CD.
- The optional SPELLING exercises provide further practice and audio links for each word and phrase.
- The exercises are designed to assist you to "see" the words you hear.

Paraphrasing Sentences:

CORRECTIONS ON PAGE 128

999. If you set up a well-run and efficient recycling scheme, there will be so little waste that you would not notice it. ***(negligible)***

There will be negligible waste that you will notice.

1000. After the divorce, the mother bought the boy a punching bag so that he didn't keep the anger which he felt toward his father inside him. ***(release)***

...so that he release the anger which he felt toward his father.

1001. I did not go down the fire-escape, or even try to get out of the building like all the other people, because I had no idea that there was, in fact, a fire. ***(aware of)***

I did not go down the fire-escape or even
because I was not aware that there was, in f

SUPERWORD #1001:

I did not go down the fire-escape, or even try to get out of the building like all the other people, because I was not aware of there being a fire.

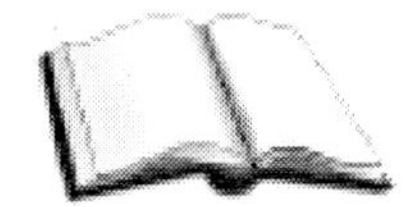

Part Three begins here in this book

PART THREE

...is your opportunity to SPEAK THE WORDS AND PHRASES you have studied with a partner – using spoken WORD PUZZLES.

- By answering each puzzle your partner provides – using the word or phrase given in the question – you will soon "own" this word!
- Fine tune your PRONUNCIATION of all the Superwords from each lesson with the optional exercises.
- Listen and immediately repeat each of the forty words and phrases of the lessons.

Spoken Word Puzzles:

1001. Many parents urge their children to study hard and to go to university rather than join the workforce as soon as they are able to leave school. Why? What are the parents **aware of** or **that**?

*The parents are **aware of** tertiary qualifications being very useful and perhaps necessary to get a good job (or "**aware that** tertiary qualifications are very useful and perhaps necessary to get a good job").*

SUGGESTED ANSWERS TO ALL PART THREE SPOKEN WORD PUZZLES CAN BE ACCESSED ONLINE.

For more details please refer to the INDEX on the CD.

turn the page for Part Three

PART 3 Lesson 1: Superwords 1~40 **Student A**

Think through the vocabulary and increase your speaking skills by taking turns at asking and answering these questions.

Try to use the lesson words as you answer.

1. The new zookeeper was fired after his first week of work. Why? Use **the performance**. What happened?

3. Can you make a statement using **generally** for each of these subjects: cats, kiwis, musicians?

5. What did he **achieve**? He was writing to apply to enter all the universities from first choice to last. He's just received a letter back and he's very happy.

7. What do you **conclude**? This is the fourth time that he's been married and each of his wives chose never to marry again.

9. She's **practically** what? She's in her fifth year at medical school? She's eight months pregnant. She's **practically** what?

11. Most people in their thirties have earned enough income to own a house and a car and to pay for a trip overseas at least twice. He rents a house but does own a car and has been overseas once, while other people have nothing. What is he **comparatively**?

13. What is his house **identical** to? He's put a high fence around his house and security light at every corner and he's got three guard dogs.

15. What did he **consume**? He could hardly stand, he sang a lot and now he cannot remember last night?

17. It is true that the present generation's lifestyle is very different from their parents' generation. Now complete this sentence. "**With regard to**...".

19. At the moment males play male sports and females play female sports. How could you **integrate** them?

21. What **accounts for** it? The streets are wet but it hasn't been raining.

23. The housewife saw some dark clouds approaching. What did it **prompt** her **to** do?

25. He **ignored** his wife. So what happened? Think of at least two ideas.

Lesson 1:
Superwords 1~40 continued...

Student A

27. They live by the bus stop. They own a car. Taxis are cheap. Their workplaces are only five and six city blocks away. So there are **several** what?

29. She believes in aliens. Why? What action did she **witness**?

31. How does an airline **allocate** seats in an aircraft? According to what?

33. Which has **the** biggest **consequences**? Getting caught stealing property (such as stationery) from your employer or getting caught shoplifting? Why do you say so?

35. In democratic countries there are elections about every three years. What does it **permit**?

37. All the children in the kindergarten went for a sleep every day at two o'clock. But one boy didn't. He continued to run around and play. Why? (Use **surplus**.)

39. This planet, unlike other planets, supports life. What is **the basis** of this support?

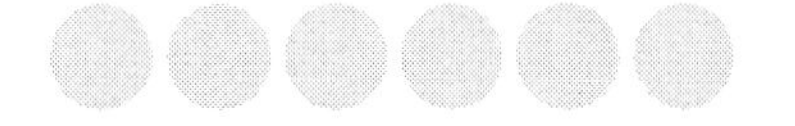

PART 3 Lesson 1: Superwords 1~40

Student B

Think through the vocabulary and increase your speaking skills by taking turns at asking and answering these questions.

Try to use the lesson words as you answer.

2. Male sports such as rugby and football are aggressive sports which result in many injuries to the players. **Meanwhile** what?

4. How did the weather **influence** the result of the football game?

6. Computer programmers are the most highly paid profession in the world. There is **a correlation** between what and what?

8. He was caught taking illegal drugs and he's just a teenager. Where did he become acquainted with them and how did he become **acquainted with** them?

10. The government has increased dog license fees by 100%. As a result, what has there been **a** higher **incidence** of?

12. What do you **attribute** it **to**? Governments in the West seldom stay in power for longer than six years.

14. What is she **particularly**? She can pick up any musical instrument and play it without a lesson.

16. Pets are great because they are excellent at keeping you company and are inexpensive to feed. Now complete this sentence: "But **in other respects**...".

18. The parents would not allow their son to watch the movie. Why? What did it **contain**?

20. Before you become a sailor, what is **vital**?

22. The boss was not paying his workers enough and then suddenly he gave them a huge raise. Why? What did the workers **threaten** the boss with? Or what did the workers **threaten** to do?

24. He stayed in the factory over night. Sometimes he did some painting and repairing. But what was he **principally** paid to do?

26. What was there **a decline** in? Women began to have fewer babies, young people went overseas for better jobs and the government cut the number of immigrants allowed into the country.

Lesson 1: Student B

Superwords 1~40 continued...

28. He'd like to be a policeman but to be a policeman **requires** what?

30. The judge sentenced the man to life in prison for murder but then **reversed** his decision. So, what exactly did the judge do? And why did he do this?

32. People who live in the Appalachian Mountains in the United States sing folk songs very similar to British folk songs from the 1800s. Can you explain? (Use **originally**.)

34. To take the perfect natural photograph of your family in a landscape, you need **favourable** conditions. What are they? Explain in detail.

36. The country would like to allow more immigrants in, but at the moment it can only **accommodate** three thousand a year. Why can it only **accommodate** this many? Think of at least three reasons.

38. After the millionaire died, he gave two thirds of his fortune to the city hospital. What did the hospital receive? (Use **substantial**.)

40. How is it that **the majority** of people can swim but **a minority** cannot?

PART 3 Lesson 2: Superwords 41~80

Student A

Think through the vocabulary and increase your speaking skills by taking turns at asking and answering these questions.

Try to use the lesson words as you answer.

41. All the planets in our solar system appear to be lifeless, **with the exception of** what?

43. All plants, and indeed life, will die if there is **an absence** of this. What is it?

45. The doctors operated on his body, after the smoker had died. What did it **confirm**?

47. 90% of households in this country have cats. 50% have dogs. Statistics were similar ten years ago. **Undoubtedly** what?

49. Recent statistics show that fewer and fewer people enjoy reading for leisure. So, what do you **predict**?

51. The student gave a reason for not doing his homework, but it was not **plausible**. What, perhaps, was his reason?

53. He had just finished working for twelve hours without a break. And the night before he had been up all night with a headache. So, what was he **immensely**?

55. He built a little hut in the forest and he covered it with leaves. He bought himself some binoculars and a notebook and pencil. Why? What did he want to **observe**?

57. Until the 1960s many people sitting in the front seats of cars in car crashes were killed. Why were there fewer killed after that? What was **the innovation**?

59. Mountain climbers seldom climb alone. And if one of them falls, he is still safe. Why? (Use **attach to**.)

61. The United States suddenly stopped spending so much money on space exploration. Why? (Use **a realisation**.)

63. When you have lost your passport, what does getting a new one **involve**?

65. If you weigh exactly the amount of food that your family will eat (the meat, the vegetables and so on), what will there be? **Minimal** what?

Lesson 2:
Superwords 41~80 continued...

Student A

67. Every time I telephoned my friend, his line was busy. And, apparently, every time he rang me, my line was busy. Why? (Use **simultaneously**.)

69. There were three applicants for the job and all had the same experience and educational qualifications. But he got the job. Why? (Use **familiar with**.)

71. She telephoned the police because she was frightened by a boy who she did not want to go out with. Why? What did he **persist in**?

73. The mailman in our suburb was not **competent**. Why not? What did he do?

75. Sometimes a government will lower taxes suddenly or spend some extra money itself on infrastructure, for example. Why? What does it want to **stimulate**?

77. The transport company said they would increase bus drivers' wages by 5%. But the drivers, who were on strike, still did not go back to work. Why? What did they **reject**? And why?

79. In each case what are they going to **adopt**? The new government is going to tax the rich more highly, just like the last government. The school is going to solve the problem of students taking drugs by doing exactly the same as a neighbouring school.

PART 3 Lesson 2: Superwords 41~80 **Student B**

Think through the vocabulary and increase your speaking skills by taking turns at asking and answering these questions.

Try to use the lesson words as you answer.

42. Why do sports players such as football players or basketball players wear different colour uniforms? "So that...". (Use **distinguish**.)

44. What does a modern home entertainment system **consist of**?

46. The nuclear power plant was immediately closed down. Why? What did scientists **detect**?

48. What do people who are travellers for their whole life never have? (Use **permanent**.)

50. He knocked at the door of every factory. He replied to every advertisement that he saw in the newspaper. He took part-time courses to upgrade his skills and qualifications? Why did he do this and what **eventually** happened?

52. The young couple dreamed of settling down. Except for clothes and food, the young couple didn't spend any money on themselves. They didn't dine out. They didn't go on holidays. They saved all their money in the bank. How was it **worthwhile**? "Not spending money...".

54. My father, who was a soldier, met my mother in 1939. They wanted to get married but they were separated for five years. Why? What **occurred**?

56. He got up at five in the morning to train. He ran twenty kilometres each morning. He spent his evenings and weekend in the gym? Why, perhaps? What was his **objective**?

58. I have a 1966 Mercedes car. I also own a 1954 Mercedes which does not go. But I keep it in my garage. Why do I keep it? (Use **interchangeable**.)

60. I had a very hard worker working for me. But, although she worked hard, she often telephoned to say she was sick or she had a problem at home. What was not **consistent** enough for me?

62. She can sing like Kiri Te Kanawa. She can dance like Ginger Rogers? She can act like Nicole Kidman. What does she have? (Use **tremendous**.)

64. If humans continue to pollute the Earth. If humans continue to wage wars. What will man **eliminate**?

Lesson 2:
Superwords 41~80 continued...

Student B

66. I often have to stand up in the bus on the way home. Why? What **exceeds** what?

68. What food is the first to **perish** when the refrigerator breaks down? Can you name three species that have **perished** or maybe are about to **perish**?

70. Leather coats are expensive and last a long time. **As opposed to** what? And how about that? "**As opposed to**... which...".

72. Why is it a good idea to put your name on the back of an envelope, before you put it in the mail? (Use **return**.) Most people can see the sense of paying tax and are in favour of it. Why? (Use **return**.)

74. Government members can go wherever they want to in the country whenever they want. How is that possible? (Use **reserve**.)

76. Why do male sportsmen always do better than women sportsmen in some games (such as rugby or football) despite the women training as much and as hard as the men. (Use **innate**.) And why do women often do better at long-distance sports? (Again, use **innate**.)

78. She was afraid of water. And she was very frightened of sharks. **Nevertheless**, what?

80. The teacher knew his subject very well. And his students usually passed their exams. However, he was not liked at all by his students. Why? What was he **overly**?

PART 3 Lesson 3: Superwords 81~120

Student A

Think through the vocabulary and increase your speaking skills by taking turns at asking and answering these questions.

Try to use the lesson words as you answer.

81. If you knew your flatmate had been wearing your clothes, what would you do? (Use **confront** and say exactly what you would do.)

83. It was very embarrassing. On his honeymoon with his new wife, who did he **encounter**? And where?

85. Only 20% of women graduating with engineering degrees get jobs compared with 60% of men. What does it **reflect**, do you think?

87. They held their wedding in the park quite soon after they fell in love, although they preferred a conventional wedding. Why? What was not **available**?

89. Even in many traditional societies women can now choose who they want to marry. Why? What is not acceptable now? (Use **the practice**...)

91. Describe the average summer holiday for people from your hometown? (Use **typically**.)

93. What are you expected to wear at a job interview? (Use **conventional** and give some examples.)

95. Why could man never live on Mars? (Explain and use **harsh**.) You should make sure you do not drop litter when you are visiting in Singapore. Why not? (Use **harsh**.)

97. He was put in charge of the running races at an international sports event. There were twenty athletes from three countries. And there were three heats leading to the finals. But he **mismanaged** it. How? What actually did he do?

99. Last year there were fifteen monkeys in the zoo. The zoo thought they were going to have to import more animals. But this year after the mating season there are twenty-nine. What is **unprecedented**?

101. It was a popular university. But this year the university made passing the final exam twice as hard as in previous years. What did it **have the effect of**?

Lesson 3:
Superwords 81~120 continued...

Student A

103. The most popular boy in school has dyed his hair pink. What do you think it will **lead to**?

105. Workers in this factory are more often absent due to sickness than any other factory. What is the Health Department going to **investigate into**?

107. Maybe he is bored. I'm thinking of taking a holiday in Australia? She could be French? It might rain. (Say these sentences again using **perhaps**.)

109. Violent programmes on television teach children how to be violent. Disagree with this statement using "**Far from ...ing,** ...".

111. You enjoy drinking a little bit of alcohol, especially with meals. It relaxes you. You are aware that not everybody uses alcohol wisely. You are talking to someone who wants alcohol completely banned. (Use **admittedly**, to explain your point of view.)

113. The rich man was dying and he was sure that he couldn't go to heaven if he owned a lot of property, possessions or money. So, what did he do? (Use **distribute**.)

115. I'm a hunter and I love shooting ducks. I was always complaining about the law that says I can only shoot them between May and July, until somebody **pointed** something **out** to me. What did he **point out**?

117. I've stopped watching the news on television, because they summarise reports on subjects such as the debate on dog control or local changes in climate. Sometimes the reports are just thirty seconds long. Instead, I read the newspaper. Why did I stop? (Use **complex**.)

119. What are **the criteria** for writing a good essay?

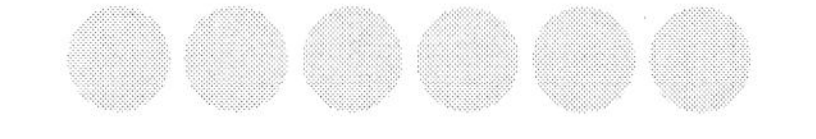

PART 3 Lesson 3: Superwords 81~120 **Student B**

Think through the vocabulary and increase your speaking skills by taking turns at asking and answering these questions.

Try to use the lesson words as you answer.

82. What is **fundamental to** a lasting relationship between a man and a woman?

84. The government broke every promise to every group of society. As a result, what was there **widespread**? "There was **widespread**…".

86. The two countries had been trading, competing in sports and had had established sister cities for many, many years. What was **historical**?

88. Nobody remembers last year's favourite pop star. What is **ephemeral**?

90. Ten years ago couples were marrying at nineteen or twenty. Five years it was more common for couples to marry at twenty-one. Statistics show that the average marrying age for young couples is now twenty-four. What is **the trend**? "There is **a trend**…".

92. What is said to be **a characteristic** of successful salesmen (insurance agents, car salesmen etc.)?

94. There are not enough trained computer technicians. So, there are many advertisements in the newspaper offering them jobs. The manager of a computer technology company wanted to **retain** his staff. So, what did he do?

96. The young boy wanted to go to a party where alcohol was being served. The parents did not want to let him go. But the young boy **assured** his parents **that**…".

98. The mother already had a very busy life. Three children to look after, a part-time job, a house to clean and maintain, and all her interests. What would **overburden** her? (Perhaps the husband wants to!)

100. She's been working as a travel agent for five years. So, she knows all about this kind of business and she has many contacts now here and overseas. And now she's begun to study business management at night school. **With a view to** what?

102. She's studying for a degree in university. Most students takes six courses each year to complete the degree in four years. But she is taking nine courses. Why? What does she want to **minimise**?

Lesson 3:

Student B

Superwords 81~120 continued...

104. The pilot was having trouble with the engines of the airplane, but he did not tell the passengers. Why not? What would it **create**?

106. The store offered a fifty percent discount on all new CD players. But **surprisingly**, what?

108. Their son is only eighteen but, despite only having a part-time job, he seems to have a lot of money. And many young people (usually untidily dressed) visit him at different hours. They leave with little parcels. What do their parents think he might be **involved in**?

110. He does not have an alarm clock or even a watch. So, what does he **rely on** to get him up on time?

112. He was the cleaner in the tourist company. But he always wore a smile, dressed tidily and spoke very politely and warmly to any customers that were passing. The company had huge growth that year because of their friendly reputation. What did the cleaner **make a contribution to**?

114. In the United States just before Thanksgiving Day, it is very hard to get tickets for flights between cities. Why? What is **the tradition** at this time?

116. Most workers came in at nine o'clock, worked all day and left at five o'clock. But he came in at eight-thirty and left at nine, returned at four forty-five and left at five fifteen again. Why? What was he employed to do? (Use **solely**.)

118. Solo parents who can get no financial help from the government or from their family, find life very hard. Why? (Use **in addition to**.)

120. There were a lot of native birds on the island. Then rats came off ships and began to kill the birds. To solve this problem, what did the government do? Now there are very few birds at all. In fact, they are almost extinct. (Explain, and then use **outnumber**.)

PART 3 Lesson 4: Superwords 121~160 — Student A

Think through the vocabulary and increase your speaking skills by taking turns at asking and answering these questions.

Try to use the lesson words as you answer.

121. Why did the traveller change his mind about changing his money to American dollars, although he was planning to go to America in a few days? (Use **current**.)

123. A stranger just opened her car door and stole the purse containing $100 when she was not there. So, it was not her fault that her money had disappeared. But what did she **acknowledge**?

125. Their parents arranged their marriage. They didn't even like each other at first. But then they learned to respect each other. What finally **developed** between them?

127. If you look at the buildings that have gone up in the last few years, you can see that many buildings have similar styles to various famous buildings built throughout history. Make a statement about this using **contemporary**.

129. Before the election the government said it had not yet finished collecting statistics on unemployment and so it had nothing to say on the subject of job losses. What did it **reveal** after the election?

131. We could solve overpopulation of the Earth by going to Mars to live. However, there are two **insurmountable** problems. What are they?

133. The athlete had a lot of will to succeed and he did succeed at the Olympics. When he was a young boy, his parents came to every competition he took part in and encouraged him in his races. What did his parents **play a role** in?

135. Soccer is the most popular amongst young children. Complete this sentence: "**Indeed**, in a poll taken last year...".

137. Who **is** always **present at** the birth of a baby? Who should **be present at** the birth of a baby? Who **is** more often **present at** the birth of a baby than twenty years ago?

139. She was allergic to dairy products such as cheese and milk. How was it **evident**?

Lesson 4:
Superwords 121~160 continued...

Student A

141. One cinema had more customers than the other cinema in town. The residents of the town did not have much money to spend on entertainment and leisure. What was the cause of the success of one cinema? (Use **–related**.)

143. It was quite surprising to the government that there were so many accidents in factories that year. So, what did it **undertake**?

145. They had a successful Internet café in the City Centre. So, they spent their profits on opening a new Internet café in the suburbs. But it was not **viable**. Why not?

147. If you own a car, you can spend a fortune each year on repairs. But what are **the alternatives**?

149. If a company cannot afford to pay workers any more money, when they are striking for better pay, of course the manager can declare that he refuses to pay any more. But what is **a** better **approach**?

151. In football or in any team sport, what can a coach do when his some of his players get tired or injured during the game. (Use **utilise**.)

153. He's a new politician but he is a very good speaker and he makes friends out of enemies easily. What has he the **potential** to do or to be? She's young. She's outgoing and she likes people. She can speak fluent English and knows Australia well (the geography, the history, the social customs). She could have a very interesting job. What? (Use **the potential**.)

155. In a job interview, what are the two most **relevant** questions that should be asked by the interviewers and what is one **irrelevant** one?

157. Even if you go overseas just to have fun, it still equips you better for life. Why? (Use **broaden**.)

159. Although the driver had only committed a minor crime (speeding), the policeman who had caught him arrested the driver and took him to the police station. Why? What had the driver **attempted**?

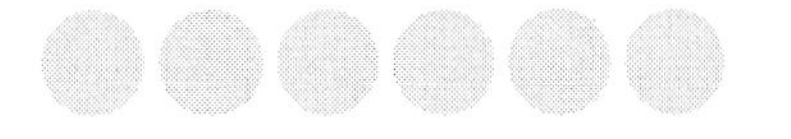

PART 3 Lesson 4: Superwords 121~160 — Student B

Think through the vocabulary and increase your speaking skills by taking turns at asking and answering these questions.

Try to use the lesson words as you answer.

122. Before the invention of the aircraft, what did not man never **conceive**?

124. Two hundred years ago people communicated long distance by only mail and letter. But what is the situation now? (Use **numerous**.)

126. There are only five Internet computers working in the school. Too many students want to use them. How did the principal **alleviate** the problem?

128. When the police find a dead body and there are no papers on the body which give the person's name. How do the police **identify** it?

130. They had a room above the stairs that was built as a study. But nobody in the large family wanted to use it for that purpose. So, what did they **convert** it **into**?

132. After the car accident, she told the police she could remember her car hitting the tree. But she could not **elaborate**. Why not?

134. What is **severe**? In Singapore you can be given a $1,000 fine just for dropping paper on the ground. What was **severe**? It was the middle of winter and in the morning the ground was all white and frozen.

136. What is **invaluable** for a businessman who has to keep a lot of appointments and go to a lot of meetings?

138. When the economy is going well, people have a lot more money to spend on dining out, going to movies and so on. So, what **flourishes** during these times?

140. The parents were in the habit of getting R18 (restricted) videos and watching them at home even when their children were there. What did they **expose** their children **to**?

142. The football fans were thrown out of the stadium. Why? Can you explain in detail? (Use **the behaviour**.) Some people believe there are aliens from other planets amongst us, but they never say hello! So, can you explain? What might be their purpose? (Again, use **the behaviour**.)

Lesson 4: Student B

Superwords 121~160 continued...

144. Complete this dialogue:

"A. Pop music is harmful for young people because it confuses them with all their messages about sex."

"B. **On the contrary**, … ."

146. The father smoked and drank all his life and then lived until he was a hundred and one. So, what was the son's **attitude** toward smoking and drinking? Both her mother and father were killed in road accidents in which the other driver was drunk. So, what was her **attitude** toward drunk-drivers?

148. His father owned a computer repair company. He was interested in computers and he used to spend Saturday mornings with his father at work. What did he **acquire**?

150. There has been a lot of information in the newspaper and on television about the numbers of older people dying from flu this winter. Many old people are alarmed by the figures. Why? **Reportedly**, what?

152. There has been a shortage of doctors this year. What **compounded** the problem?

154. It is a double-decker bus. There are forty seats downstairs and thirty seats upstairs. Including the bus driver, what **capacity** does the bus **have**?

156. He drove his neighbour to work when his neighbour's car broke down. When his colleague at work was sick, he visited him and took groceries too. What does he **readily** do?

158. In the past the government used to promote people according to how long the person had served in the government department. In other words, it promoted people **irrespective** of what?

160. I told my wife that we should hire caregivers for our children so that she could go back to work. But she disagreed. What did she **argue**?

PART 3 Lesson 5: Superwords 161~200

Student A

Think through the vocabulary and increase your speaking skills by taking turns at asking and answering these questions.

Try to use the lesson words as you answer.

161. In the hotel all the clients had to wear their coats inside. Why? What was **inadequate**?

163. He was very tired but she could not sleep all night. Why not? (Use **continuously**.)

165. On what **occasion** is it traditional for Western people to wear black clothes?

167. He was not violent to his wife. But he complained to her all the time and said negative things about her personality to her for years. What did this **constitute**?

169. An entertainment area including bars is being built beside the school. Why is this **of concern**?

171. Who do drug traffickers try to sell their drugs to? Who is **vulnerable** to it and why?

173. Describe **the process** of getting a license to drive a car.

175. When he saw the young girl drowning in the lake, what did he **endeavour to** do? And what happened in the end?

177. People who exercise and eat a good diet and live good lives do **not necessarily** what?

179. When the old man died they gave his dog to a little boy in a neighbouring town. But the dog loved the master very much and was very loyal. So, what did the dog **repeatedly** do?

181. She liked to listen to other people's conversations. At the outdoor café, she could hear the conversation of the couple at the next table, but she couldn't **comprehend** it. Why not?

183. He had no **means of** getting to work at all that day. Why not?

185. It was a small Pacific Ocean island. Its highest point was just ten metres above sea level. What **devastated** it?

187. He had a **disastrous** day at the gambling casino. What happened?

Lesson 5:
Superwords 161~200 continued...

Student A

189. The company manager did not want to lay off 50% of his workers during the economic downturn. But what was his **priority**?

191. When local people could not buy meat because the meat companies were sending all their produce overseas to better paying markets, what **measures** did the government **take to** solve the problem?

193. He was worried about her health. She had had a cold for weeks. She visited two doctors, but they gave **conflicting** advice. What was their advice actually?

195. Cars cause huge amounts of pollution which makes people sick. It has been estimated that millions of dollars are lost out of the economy due to this sickness. Fewer cars and more buses would result in much less pollution and sickness. Most people say they cannot afford to travel in buses. (Make a logical concluding sentence using ... **, then,** ... .)

197. He can speak six languages **including** what? (Clue: five of the languages are second languages to him.)

199. This country is 1,200 kilometres long. If you decided to walk that distance, how much time do you think it would take? Why do you say this much? (Use **estimate**.)

PART 3 Lesson 5: Superwords 161~200

Student B

Think through the vocabulary and increase your speaking skills by taking turns at asking and answering these questions.

Try to use the lesson words as you answer.

162. If you want to find out where is the best place to invest your savings in the bank, who do you **consult**? If your marriage is not going very well, who do you **consult**?

164. He made a lot of money on the money markets. The Australian government had announced that they expected higher unemployment and a rise in the cost of living over the coming three months. How did he make his money on the money markets? (Use **speculate**.)

166. The school had both boy and girl students. Most of the teachers were males over forty years of age. Fortunately, at the end of the year half of these teachers decided to leave. In the new year, how did the school **counterbalance** the male teachers who were over forty years of age?

168. The parents were unhappy because dogs were defecating on the beach. So, the council put up signs on the beach front. What did the signs say, perhaps? (Use **prohibit**.)

170. When he shared ownership of the company with two other people, he always had to hold meetings with his partners before making important business decisions. But then he bought his partners' shares. What did he **obtain** when he did this, because he no longer has to consult his partners?

172. Describe him. He never says "please" or "thank you". And when people say "hi", he often just ignores them. He never joins queues. He just goes straight to the counter to get served. (Use **extremely**.)

174. What did it **highlight**? The tourist brochure reported that the country had the third lowest crime rate in the world and it reported the high temperatures of summer but nothing about the exchange rate or the price of everyday commodities.

176. His wife was going out for two hours every night, without saying where she was going. He thought she had a boyfriend. So, he hired a private detective to follow her. But the news from the private detective was good. What did the private detective **ascertain**?

178. He never goes to concerts. He never boards buses at peak times. Why? What can't he **tolerate**?

Lesson 5: Student B

Superwords 161~200 continued...

180. Rabbits were eating his vegetables in his vegetable garden. How did he **counter** them?

182. Everybody wants to work for the movies. When the movie makers came to town, they put an advertisement in the town offering jobs for extras and for labourers. What were they **inundated with**?

184. She could pick up any musical instrument and begin to play it (although she had had no training in playing it). She could listen to a piece of music for a few seconds, and then begin to play it accurately. What was **exceptional**?

186. He didn't study very hard, but he had a lot of success at school. He seemed to know what the teachers were going to test him. He also organised his time and wrote just enough words when he was being tested. What was he **adept at**?

188. There were huge forest fires in the country that year. Most of the trees had been grown to produce paper for newspapers and magazines. What was the result of the fire? Describe the situation using **resultant**. (Begin: "There were huge forest fires in the country that year...".)

190. He goes out in all kinds of weather in his boat and he never wears a life jacket. What is **bound to** happen sooner or later?

192. He was sixteen and had just bought his first second-hand car. His father was a mechanic. What could he **assist** his son to do?

194. What do pillows, a mattress, blankets, sheets, springs and headboards **comprise**?

196. The government was going to tax him highly because of all the money he had saved in the bank. But he managed to escape the tax by **disposing of** his money. What did he do with it, do you think?

198. That hot summer there was not enough water for drinking or washing. Yet many households were using water wastefully for many purposes around the house. So, the government acted. What did it do exactly? (Use **legislate**.)

200. Recent statistics show that 90% of criminals commit crimes again after prison. However, statistics also show that the second crime is 100% worse than the first one. So, what are many people **debating**?

PART 3 Lesson 6: Superwords 201~240

Student A

Think through the vocabulary and increase your speaking skills by taking turns at asking and answering these questions.

Try to use the lesson words as you answer.

201. He received a letter from the Tax Department. He felt worried as a result. What did it inform him, perhaps. (Use **inform**.)

203. I don't know my neighbours very well, but I do know they **originated from** Holland. How do I know?

205. It has been said that the rules of football are too hard for even the players to understand. So, the rules should be **simplified**. Can you **simplify** them?

207. The security guard rushed out of the bank. Why? What was he **pursuing**? The couple decided not to have children at all. Why? What were they **pursuing**?

209. What does central heating automatically **adjust** these days to keep a constant environment? When the new set of traffic lights made the buses arrive later, what had to be **adjusted**?

211. Look up the meaning of "plagiarism" in an English–English dictionary and make a sentence using **defined as**. Then, according to this definition, give one example of plagiarism by a student and another example of non-plagiarism by a student.

213. The colour of her house was **unique**. What colour was it? Her hairstyle was **unique**. What was it like? She had a tattoo on a **unique** place. Where was it?

215. Eating much more food than you need (especially when you know there are hungry people in the world) **amounts to** what?

217. It is quite difficult for women who have been raising children for five years or more to be fully employed in the workforce. So what could be a **transition**?

219. Her grandmother lived in a nearby town. But she did not know her grandmother very well at all. Why not? (Use **rarely**.)

221. The roof was leaking and the water was damaging all the furniture. But they did not have very much money to repair it. So, what was the **short-term** solution and what was the **long-term** one?

Lesson 6: Student A

Superwords 201~240 continued...

223. Right-wing members of the government were against allowing new immigrants into the country. When refugees came across the border to live in the country, what did these politicians **advocate**?

225. What will be the result of a society educating its children well, do you think? (Use **to... , is to...** in your answer.)

227. Use **as... , so...** to express these truths: during the winter, the shorter the day is, the colder the temperature is. A worker will work harder if he is given more responsibility.

229. Cartoon books are enjoyed even by very young children and by people who have not had a very good education. (Explain this situation using **whether**.)

231. His father owns a shipping empire and he is the only son. So, what is he **destined to** become?

233. She was very talented at music, but she knew that it was hard to make a living out of it. Thus, when she went to university, she studied sciences and maths. However, she failed all of her exams. **In retrospect**, what?

235. Crime was going up hugely. So, to act against it, what did the government **boost**?

237. It is true that most women reach maturity sooner than men, (women in their early twenties and men in their late twenties). So, what **phenomenon** does this truth explain? **The phenomenon** of...?

239. The company was successful because it made the public know about its products through the television, newspapers and large posters. So what could we say? What was **pivotal to** the company's success?

PART 3 Lesson 6: Superwords 201~240

Student B

Think through the vocabulary and increase your speaking skills by taking turns at asking and answering these questions.

Try to use the lesson words as you answer.

202. If my neighbour needs a ride to work, I'll offer to take him. If a stranger comes up to me on the street and ask for money, I'll give him some. What is my **philosophy**?

204. More and more of the buildings on the block became shops, and after a while they put a roof over them all. What did the city block **evolve from** and into?

206. When he was young he kept records in his diary. And then he composed poetry and wrote short stories which he published. Critics said he was certain to write a great novel one day, but he never did. What **stagnated**?

208. Millions of years ago, possibly after meteors hit the Earth and made the world freeze, what well-known creatures **vanished** from the Earth?

210. He gave me all his personal details including his name and address and so on, but when I tried to telephone him, I could not contact him. Why not? (Use **correct**.)

212. You will never feel down or sad or want to give up, if you **focus on** this. What is it?

214. The law in this country says that if an employee makes a serious mistake, he must be given a second chance, and the employer must first give the employee the opportunity to improve his performance. But **in practice** what happens?

216. Where are koalas **confined to**? Where are kiwis **confined to**? And where are panda bears **confined to**?

218. In the classroom what behaviour by the teacher is **unacceptable**?

220. Although adventure sports companies want most of all to provide excitement for their customers, to make them feel better, what do these companies tell the customers that the **emphasis** is **on**?

222. **Precisely** when does a new year begin?

224. In most western countries, everybody has the freedom to do whatever he or she likes **unless** what?

Lesson 6:
Superwords 201~240 continued...
Student B

226. You could call karate and judo very violent sports. Yet these sports do not seem to cause as many injuries as in rugby or boxing. Why not? (Use **though**.) Begin: "Karate and judo are very violent sports like rugby and boxing. ...".

228. If you drink too much alcohol at a party, you might not be able to stand up. What else might not be possible? (Use **nor**... .)

230. A lot of paper and pens were disappearing from the office. One of the workers always came in early and left late and he always carried a rather large briefcase. What did the boss **suspect**?

232. One of the politicians suggested to the government that it get the country out of economic trouble by raising taxes by 25%. But what was this **dismissed as**?

234. He was a very rich man with only one son. So, of course he planned to leave all of his wealth to his son when he died. But when he found out that his son had been dishonest and had cheated him, he spoke to his lawyer. What did he say exactly? (Use **instruct**.)

236. If competition is removed from the market; for example, if there is only one airline operating in the country, what **soars**?

238. Many office workers these days are getting injuries to the muscles in their hands and fingers from exercising them in the office too much. What actually is **the culprit**?

240. It is true that travelling by car can make you late when you get caught in a traffic jam. And when they occasionally break down, you can wait hours waiting for a mechanic to rescue you. But **overall** what and why?

PART 3 Lesson 7: Superwords 241~280

Student A

Think through the vocabulary and increase your speaking skills by taking turns at asking and answering these questions.

Try to use the lesson words as you answer.

241. He was overweight but he reduced his food intake to one meal a day for three months. What happened afterwards? (Use **as a result of**... .)

243. He needed to study for one more year at university. To do what? (Use **complete**.) He needed to find the word for one more clue? To **complete** what?

245. When it was announced that the price of petrol was going up, everybody went out and bought some. What was this **the cause** of?

247. She was only nineteen and she announced to her parents that she was going on a hitch-hiking tour of India by herself and, of course, she had the right to do so. But the parents were worried, so what did they **urge** her to do?

249. The airliner crashed killing 150 passengers because it ran out of fuel. In your opinion, who (if anyone) should be blamed for the accident and why? (Use **responsible for**.)

251. What can having too many children too soon **have an adverse effect on**?

253. The mother was a solo parent who found a boyfriend and got married. When her daughter got to know his mother's new husband, what did she **regard** him **as**?

255. Although he didn't need the money, he decided to sell his car. Why? (Use **seldom**.)

257. He was sure his son would not be able to finish the marathon, but he did. What did the father **misjudge**?

259. A lot of the soldiers in the army, who were less than courageous, decided to quit. Why? What wãs **impending**?

261. At last the young man got a job. But he had to start work at four o'clock in the morning. And his place of work was distant. What probably **posed** a problem?

263. The overseas student telephoned her mother, but the mother still complained that she missed her daughter. Why? What was **intermittent**?

Lesson 7:
Superwords 241~280 continued...

Student A

265. Even though the boss and the workers reached agreement about the wages, two months later the workers still went out on strike. Why? What did the boss not **deliver**?

267. He worked as a maths teacher but he played the guitar very well. What was his **secondary** job?

269. Although she loved her husband very much, she decided to divorce him. Why? What did she **discover**?

271. She was very keen to keep her job and even hoped to be promoted. So, what did she do to **impress** her boss?

273. To be a doctor you cannot be afraid of blood. You must be interested in the body and be a careful and caring person. But what else does it require? (Use **some**.)

275. He needs 108 points to get a degree. He can take six courses each year, and each of them is worth six points. So, what did he **calculate**?

277. He's a millionaire and he's **merely** what? She was drinking in a hotel and she was **merely** what?

279. How tall is your teacher? How many people live in this city? How many movies have you been to this year? (Use **approximately**.)

PART 3 Lesson 7: Superwords 241~280

Student B

Think through the vocabulary and increase your speaking skills by taking turns at asking and answering these questions.

Try to use the lesson words as you answer.

242. What is the most **catastrophic** event caused by mankind, do you think? Explain your reason.

244. In what ways are telephones more **sophisticated** than they were ten years ago, or even five years ago, or even two years ago?

246. If you bring a new pet into the house, how do the older pets **interact with** it? How do people out on a blind date usually **interact**?

248. He was against prisons as a form of punishment, because he did not think that they successfully corrected criminal behaviour. This was his argument. But he was a reasonable man and when you discussed the issue of the need for prisons with him, what did he **concede**?

250. He was a lawyer. And twice in his experience, convicted killers were sentenced to death and too late it was discovered that they did not commit the crimes at all. So, what was he **opposed to**?

252. What **breakthrough** is necessary if humans are to live forever? What **breakthrough** was needed over a hundred years ago so that people could travel from America to Britain in a few hours?

254. He didn't have much money and he did not know which was cheaper – to travel home to his city by bus or by train. So, who did he telephone and what did he **inquire into**?

256. His children had gone into the forest for a walk four hours ago and it would be dark in two hours. He was worried, so he telephoned the police who **initiated** what?

258. He was the only fisherman who went to sea that morning and got caught in the storm. Why? What did he not **attend to**?

260. Although he owned his own house and a yacht, the bank manager refused to grant him a loan. Why? What was **deficient**?

262. He was a hardworking clerk in the company. And when the receptionist left, he wanted her job. But the boss would not give him the job. Why not? What were his **shortcomings**?

Lesson 7: Student B
Superwords 241~280 continued...

264. The apes might control the planet (or the insects in their large numbers might control the planet) if what happened? (Use **humanity**.)

266. His hobby was collecting stamps, but his collection was rather **random**? What was in it?

268. When you go to a museum, you see many things that are not used so much now. What do these things **date back to**? Candlestick holders; spears; sewing machines; pen portraits of family members. (Begin: "They **date back to** a time when...".)

270. He has been married three times and divorced three times. All of his marriages have been unhappy. Yet he has decided to get married again. What has he **succumbed to**?

272. She does not allow her daughter to even touch a cigarette. She has asked the owner of the local shop to take down his posters advertising cigarettes. She writes to her representative in government regularly to ask him to enact strict laws about it. What is she **anti-**? What is she **pro-**?

274. Last year the country had a major earthquake. It was followed by a severe drought. And then in April came the monsoons and the floods. What has the country experienced? (Use **a series**.)

276. He has set himself a goal of being promoted to manager of the company within two years. But it is **unrealistic**. Why is it **unrealistic**?

278. The judges in Western courts usually give the mother possession of the children after a divorce. They do that **on** what **premise**?

280. When her friends asked her about the language school she attended, she **criticized** it. What actually did she say, do you think?

PART 3 Lesson 8: Superwords 281~320

Student A

Think through the vocabulary and increase your speaking skills by taking turns at asking and answering these questions.

Try to use the lesson words as you answer.

281. Women are often given the children by the courts after a divorce. Most accidents with children in the home happen when the father is in charge. What do these facts **exemplify**?

283. A carpenter needs a saw, a plane, and a drill **as well as** what?

285. Mobile phones, emails, text messaging are commonly used nowadays. Now make a sentence beginning "**Such**... ".

287. Cities are stimulating and entertaining places. But what **detracts from** this excitement?

289. Less and less will have to be done by humans in the workplace but especially in factories. **With** the com**ing** of what?

291. His mother did not recognize her own son when she met him at the railway station. Why? What had **radically** changed? And give an example.

293. He usually catches the bus at eight o'clock to get to work. Now, the bus company has changed the schedule. The bus will leave at seven forty-five. For him, what does this **mean**?

295. He was planning to go overseas to study. He preferred to go to the United States to study rather than Australia, but what were **the obstacles**?

297. The English Language School had an Open Day. People interested in studying at the school could be shown around. On the Open Day there were English language teachers there from England, Australia and the United States. But it was just **a façade**. Explain how it was **a façade**.

299. A football team can exercise, develop its skills, practise a great deal and plan, but on match day what is the team never truly **confident** that?

301. Mountaineering can be a very dangerous sport. Use this fact to add information. (Use **as is the case with...** and **this is not the case with...** .)

303. The father had been in prison for being violent after drinking too much alcohol. The local welfare agency thought his children might be **at risk**. Why? What did they think?

Lesson 8: Student A

Superwords 281~320 continued...

305. Last century, wars in Europe were very common. **Unlike** where? Beer is a very mild kind of alcohol. **Unlike** what? Overseas travel is affordable to most young people these days. **Unlike** who?

307. When the woman went overseas, she employed a local teenager to look after her house and everything in and around it. When she returned, she found the house was very clean and the garden was very tidy. But her cat was thin and all the house plants were dead. Why? (Use **neglect**.)

309. A dead body was found in a car. His body was not bruised and his arms and legs were not broken. And there was not any blood. Yet he was dead. Can you explain? (Use **external** or **internal**.)

311. Morphine is an illegal drug. But, of course, certain people are **exempt**. Who are they and why are they **exempt**?

313. The student told her parents that she unfortunately did not pass the examination, because she had made stupid mistakes on the examination paper. This was not true. (Use **actual** to explain.)

315. He was unmarried and his friends were always finding him girlfriends to go out with. He liked many of them; their personalities and their appearances. But he never ever married. Why? (Use **simply**.)

317. She could draw and paint very, very well. Her portraits of people were absolutely lifelike. But she was shy and she painted pictures only of her friends. Also she refused to sell her pictures on the market. Why? (Use **display**.)

319. She always had a breathing problem. It came from a childhood illness in her lungs. And then she moved to the big city and her breathing problem became worse. Why? What **aggravated** it?

PART 3 Lesson 8: Superwords 281~320

Student B

Think through the vocabulary and increase your speaking skills by taking turns at asking and answering these questions.

Try to use the lesson words as you answer.

282. What's the best thing to do with rubbish, so that it does not **endanger** the environment?

284. She heard that her place of work was closing down, and, with three children, she could not afford to be without work. So, what did she immediately **explore**?

286. If the government becomes conservative and bans sex education and contraceptives, what problems will **emerge**? If you feel angry but keep it inside, what problems will probably **emerge**?

288. Alcohol is the most commonly used drug in society, but it is not at all the safest. In fact...what? (Use **amongst**.)

290. They say, compared wth Asian societies, young women in the West have a lot more freedom. What is **the extent** of their freedom? Or what is **the extent** of the lack of freedom of Asian young women?

292. The student could not understand the lesson and so she asked the teacher questions afterwards. He gave her an explanation but she still did not fully understand. She wanted more explanation. So, what question did she ask? "Excuse me, but... ." (Use **further**.)

294. He worked for a school as a repairman and he was a very **versatile** handyman? Why? What could he do?

296. He went walking through the hills and mountains. He got caught in the rain and got pneumonia. And he lost his directions and took three days to find his way. Why? What two things was he not **equipped with**?

298. The young man's main interest was not study but surfing, and he spent ninety percent of his time at the beach. His father managed to persuade him to study harder and pass his university entrance exams. How? (Use **the incentive**.)

300. Do you think it is **naïve** to accept a "free" taxi service from the airport to the City Centre? Explain why or why not using **naïve**. Do you think it is **naïve** to buy second hand goods when they are almost new and are 90% cheaper than the new price? Again, explain why or why not using **naïve**.

Lesson 8:
Superwords 281~320 continued...

Student B

302. The father was playing football in the backyard in the evening with his son when the ball went over the fence into his neighbour's property. The father jumped the fence to get the ball back. The neighbour saw him and immediately telephoned the police. Why? (Use **mistaken for**.)

304. This year young people are wearing baggy jeans and bright-coloured tops. Last year they wore tight shorts with long shirts over top. In other words, what **varies**?

306. For a month at work, while her manager was away sick, she was paid a lot more and she told the other workers what to do. Why? (Use **temporarily**.)

308. The busy mother, wife and worker had many bills to pay each month – electricity, telephone and rent. But she never had to remember to pay them. Why not? (Use **automatically**. *Clue: it is about the bank.*)

310. He was overweight and had heart problems. What two things did his doctor say will be **beneficial**?

312. During the winter months, the chemist shops get very busy. Why? (Use **a demand**.)

314. He ran and owned a transport company. One Friday he made sure all of his trucks and cars were filled with petrol or diesel fuel. Why? What did he **anticipate**? What was he able to do as a result?

316. I have a friend who does not own a thing – not a house, not a car, only two sets of clothes. He shares everything with everybody. I have another friend who is almost a millionaire. We go out to dinner together, but he never offers to pay. I'm afraid it is true. "**The more**.... ." (Complete the sentence.)

318. The young thirteen year-old boy wants $80 from his mother to buy a toy remote-control car. The mother won't give him $80, but what is she **willing to** do?)

320. Can you explain? In the country, when you look up at the sky you can see millions of stars. In the city, when you look up at the sky you usually cannot see a single star. Why not? (Use **whereas**.)

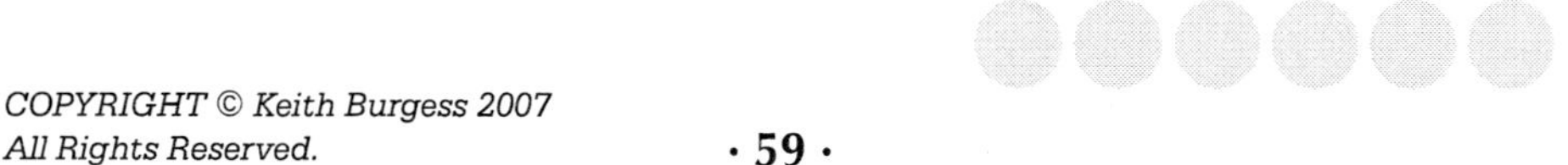

PART 3 Lesson 9: Superwords 321~360

Student A

Think through the vocabulary and increase your speaking skills by taking turns at asking and answering these questions.

Try to use the lesson words as you answer.

321. When a child does something well, she will try to do even better if her mother **rewards** her **with** what?

323. The airline company had a plan to decrease costs by having just one pilot instead of two on each flight. But why could it not **implement** the plan?

325. He set up a restaurant in the busy part of the city. But all the other restaurants were chain restaurants and were cheaper. So, what did he **struggle to** do?

327. The students were protesting violently in the City Centre against the huge increase in tuition fees and other government policies. The government brought in the army as well as the police to **restore** what?

329. The patient was very sick. Three organs (his heart, his liver and his kidney) were not working. But the doctor had an **ambitious** plan. What was it?

331. He lost his job after fifteen years in a factory. Why did he **welcome** it?

333. The company introduced a rule that smoking was not allowed in the offices or in the workers cafeteria. Why did the workers not **comply with** it?

335. He never wore shorts in public. Why? What was he **conscious of**?

337. In some countries, buildings never have a thirteenth floor. In Western countries, number seven is the most popular number in gambling. What is **curious**?

339. The five-year-old child was much thinner than other children her age. Why? What was she **under-**...?

341. When is a low tax and a strong social welfare system not **sustainable**?

343. When the couple found out that they could not, unfortunately, have children, what were their **options**?

345. He entered a dancing competition. But to win, he had to **perfect** his steps. How did he do it?

Lesson 9: Student A
Superwords 321~360 continued...

347. The elementary school was an old brick building. When the earthquake began to shake thebuilding, what were the teachers **anxious to** do?

349. Even when you are very thirsty, you should not drink sea water. Why not? What will you **ingest**?

351. At the beginning of the course on statistics there were two hundred students. At the beginning of the second semester there were only one hundred. And at the end of the course there were fifty students left. Can you explain? (Use **progressively**.)

353. Her husband never remembers her birthday now. If he is coming home late, he never telephones to let her know. He didn't comment on her new dress. What is **apparent** to her?

355. Her fifteen-year-old daughter wanted to go to a party until two o'clock in the morning. Did the mother say "yes" or "no"? And what was the mother **prepared to** do?

357. He thought the documentary on the ancient history would be very boring. But the film contained a lot of amazing facts he did not know. What did the documentary **prove to be**?

359. The farm is very near the city. The farm has over a thousand sheep. The farmer's fences are not very good. In fact, some of them are broken. Why is this **hazardous**?

PART 3 Lesson 9: Superwords 321~360

Student B

Think through the vocabulary and increase your speaking skills by taking turns at asking and answering these questions.

Try to use the lesson words as you answer.

322. If you take small things home from the company that do not belong to you – such as pens and paper and spare floppy discs – what do you **jeopardize** and why?

324. The house which he was renting was sold to another landlord. Two weeks after that, he decided to leave the house and rent another (even though he was comfortable there). Why did he do this? **In response to** what?

326. To solve the problem of overcrowding in the city, the government made a law which limited each family to two-room apartments. But what was the government looking at **in isolation**?

328. The average rent for a small apartment is $200 a week. It costs the average family $150 a week for food, $40 for clothing and $100 for everything else. Their family income was $495 a week. Make a statement using **barely**.

330. He was a smart young lawyer and the law firm wanted him. So, they agreed to pay him $1,000, buy him a car, and pay for an overseas holiday each year. But after a year he was disappointed and decided to leave. Why? (Use **fulfil**.)

332. If you are a taxi driver, what **expertise** do you need? If you are a marriage counsellor, what **expertise** do you need?

334. The government has limited money to spend on health care. In your opinion, what **sections** of society should it look after first?

336. In your opinion, how many holidays are **sufficient** each year? How many days off each week are **sufficient**? Why do you say so?

338. Look at a map of the world. What does South East Asia **encompass**?

340. Margaret and Colin both study psychology. As part of their study, they were asked to investigate into the reasons that people smoke. Margaret got A plus for her work, while Colin just got B. Why was his work considered **inferior**?

342. The motorist accidentally hit a boy on a bicycle. The punishment for this is usually a very heavy fine. But this motorist was sent to prison. Why? What had he **failed to** do?

Lesson 9: Student B
Superwords 321~360 continued...

344. What age groups are **the domain** of... a) nightclubs, b) shopping malls, c) golf courses, and d) skateboard parks?

346. The hospital knows that visitors are good for patients. So the hospital is fairly open-minded about the number and times of visits by the family and friends of patients. But they had to have some rules. What did it do? (Use **set parameters** with details.)

348. What is your favourite dish and what are **the ingredients**? In your opinion, what are **the ingredients** of a good novel?

350. The accountant of his company, who looked after all its money, did not pay any of the company's bills for months. So, what did his company **accumulate**?

352. He knew a lot of people who liked to jog just to keep fit or for fun. So, what did they **form**?

354. Although transport is expensive, fruit and vegetables are three times more expensive in the city than in the countryside. Describe this situation using **disproportionately**.

356. Two men took part in the robbery. But one man (aged thirty-four) was sentenced to five years in prison by the courts, while the other (aged twenty-two) was sentenced to only three years in prison. Why? What did the court **deem**?

358. When he saw that the rail bridge had collapsed, he ran down the railway track to stop the train. Thus, what did he **avert**?

360. If the population of this country was two and a half million one hundred years ago and now it is seven and a half million, what could we say about the population change? (Use **–fold**.)

PART 3 Lesson 10: Superwords 361~400

Student A

Think through the vocabulary and increase your speaking skills by taking turns at asking and answering these questions.

Try to use the lesson words as you answer.

361. Today 30,000 workers without jobs marched to the government buildings and protested. Why? What had the government not **addressed**?

363. If scientists can find a pill that will keep us healthy for life, what might become **obsolete**?

365. The cows in the country caught a terrible disease that year, and one half of them had to be killed and their bodies burnt. So, what was there **a shortage** of that year?

367. There were eighteen players in the top team of the football club. Of course, only eleven players could play. He had an outstanding game and scored four wonderful goals. What did he **secure**?

369. It is a very big university and teaches just about every subject that universities can teach. (Use **range from... to...** to describe this fact.)

371. When the fire alarm sounds in an office building, who is expected to **assemble** and where?

373. He lost his passport. Why was it **inconsequential**? His neighbour died. Why was it **inconsequential**? He was arrested for thieving, but why was it **inconsequential**?

375. Based on where you are living right now, what is the area called **locally**? What is the area called **nationally**? What is the area called **regionally**?

377. We were going to go fishing at sea, but what **arose** so we decided we had better not?

379. What do Asian students **tend to** study at English-speaking universities and why? And who are the exceptions?

381. She loved her son. Her son was arrested for theft. There was a lot of evidence against him. But the mother loved her son very much indeed and did not want to lose him to prison. So, what belief did she **adhere to**?

383. If you are sending an expensive gift in the mail, what **precaution** should you **take**?

Lesson 10:
Superwords 361~400 continued...

Student A

385. What is **disruptive** on the highway in the early morning rush? And why?

387. He sent an order for a book to a mail order company, but he never ever received it. Why not? What did he **omit**?

389. When she chooses a sports team to join at the beginning of each year, she researches the team's performance first. Nobody else does this. In addition to training, she goes jogging every night and works out in the gym on Saturday and Sunday. No other player does this. When the score of the first game was twenty-five – zero to the other team, she broke down and cried. Why? Can you explain all this? What is she **obsessed with**?

391. Who do workers **negotiate with** and about what? Who can policemen **negotiate with** and about what? Who can lawyers **negotiate with** and about what?

393. What is **a feature** in Paris? What is **a feature** of McDonalds that is not **a feature** of KFC? What is **a feature** of law students?

395. The year is 2003. Think about transport. What is it **the era** of? Think about music. What is it **the era** of? Think about world politics. What is it **the era** of?

397. She is against immigration being allowed to increase. Why? What does she **assert**? He's in favour of young men being made to join the army. Why? What does he **assert**?

399. If the population of a species is a hundred individuals, what are they **apt to** do?

PART 3 Lesson 10: Superwords 361~400

Student B

Think through the vocabulary and increase your speaking skills by taking turns at asking and answering these questions.

Try to use the lesson words as you answer.

362. Because of the air pollution, the council wants households to use electric heaters more than wood or coal burners. So, what could be their **strategy**?

364. For years he played his guitar and sang in bars. He often sent his music to record companies, but they ignored it. Now, he has been offered a record contract and the record company is going to advertise his CD worldwide. What does he seem to be **on the verge of**?

366. He used to think that women belonged in the kitchen or at least at home looking after children. Now he admires their keen business sense and has hired mainly women to run his company. What has been **transformed**?

368. He believed in low taxes for the benefit of the economy. When the government lowered taxes and years later the economy was booming, what did this **reinforce**?

370. Recently a way has been **devised** to have fewer prisons and yet keep all criminals away from society. What is it?

372. This week I drank no beer at all. Last week I drank three bottle of beer. The previous week, I had friends staying and we had a party, so I drank nine bottles of beer that week. We could say "**On average,** ..." what?

374. A poll was taken. 50% of the people said that they were in favour of going to war with the United States in Iraq. Just as many people (50%) were opposed to the idea. Describe this situation. (Use **divide**.)

376. Conservative-thinking people want murderers to be imprisoned for a long time, **preferably** how long? On the other hand, liberal-thinking people want criminals like these to be given a chance to improve themselves, **preferably** where?

378. After the bank robbery, the bank robber saw his picture on television and knew he would be caught. So what did he **voluntarily** do?

380. Only half of the students at morning break time were able to have white coffee. Why? What was **scarce**? 70% of graduate students in this country go overseas to live. Why? What is **scarce**?

Lesson 10: Student B
Superwords 361~400 continued...

382. The doctor told his patient that he had to give up smoking. After the consultation, the receptionist at the doctors **undermined** his advice? How? What did she do?

384. The result of his exam was satisfactory. What percentage did he get? The motel room and its facilities were **satisfactory**. What were they like actually?

386. When you get married and have children, what is your **obligation**? When a bank lends you money, what is your **obligation**? When an employee has been working for a company for years and decides to leave, what is his **obligation**?

388. Prisons are often built in **remote** locations. Why is this so? Engineers often have to work in **remote** locations. Again, why is this so?

390. In your opinion, who is **discriminated against** the most in the workplace? Women, disabled people, the elderly, or people from foreign cultures. Explain your choice.

392. Which jobs in your society have **the** highest **status**? Which jobs have **the** lowest **status**? Explain how this is so.

394. The hospitals cannot afford to hire any more doctors. There are not enough beds for patients. Patients are being charged for medicine. What needs to be **injected** into the health system?

396. He has successfully graduated from high school. So, what is he **eligible to** do? He is single and over twenty-one. So, what is he **eligible to** do?

398. He thinks every citizen should be able to protect himself in the street or at home with weapons. So, what is he **an opponent** of?

400. The beaches and the little coastal towns on the French Riviera are very popular holiday spots in the summertime. So, what are these places **invaded** with?

PART 3 Lesson 11: Superwords 401~440

Student A

Think through the vocabulary and increase your speaking skills by taking turns at asking and answering these questions.

Try to use the lesson words as you answer.

401. Students at the College used to be able to choose any courses and so most of the students took business courses. But now students must take three arts or science courses. Why does the College have this rule? (Use **imbalance** and explain.)

403. New Zealand is a country which is completely surrounded by ocean. Complete this statement. "**By contrast**... ".

405. His taxi business was not making enough money because it was not the busy season. He needed money to pay next month's rent. He had a mother and father in the same city. He'd been banking with the same bank for ten years. He had some good friends he'd known since childhood. And he had a car worth $20,000. What did he decide to do? And what did he **discount** doing and why?

407. He saw a mother hitting her child in the supermarket, but he did not intervene. Why not? Two gang members were fighting with knives in the car park, but he did not **intervene**? Why not? An old lady was struggling with a kid who was trying to steal her handbag in the park. So, he **intervened**. Why?

409. When the doctor was carrying out the heart operation, what did he **inadvertently** do?

411. Doctors should not be emotional about their patients, but this doctor is especially **despondent about** his patient. Why?

413. Cats come over the fence to my house, and they dig up all the plants. What could be **a deterrent**?

415. His wife loved children and wanted another baby. But he said "no" because he wanted to have money for a car and later a new house. Why did he say "no". (Use **materialism**.)

417. It is expected that inflation will rise significantly next year. His boss gave him a bonus of $10,000. What is it **prudent** for him to do?

419. It is fifty years in the future. And nobody can drive their cars. Why? What has been **exhausted**?

Lesson 11: Student A

Superwords 401~440 continued...

421. He love animals of every kind. He has a horse a goat, three cats and even has a camel. What does his house **resemble**?

423. Robbing the bank was easy for him because he knew where they kept the money and he knew where the cameras and alarms were set. Why was it easy? What was he **formerly**?

425. When the boss asked him where they should have the annual Christmas party, he suggested a picnic in the park. But actually he was **indifferent about** the location of the party. Why?

427. Because of high unemployment and to share the work around, the government wants employers to reduce the working week to thirty hours (and, of course, still pay them the same). How could the government **facilitate** this?

429. Everybody thinks the police were too **lenient** with drink drivers twenty years ago. Why? What did they do then?

431. Most adults know that guns are dangerous, but many children do not. Yet, on television in many violent programmes we can see people being shot and surviving. (They stand up and walk away!) What do these programmes **perpetuate**?

433. She was nineteen (a teenager still) but she was about to finish her study, begin her first job, stop living with her parents, and perhaps get married soon. In fact, her world was about to change forever. Describe this situation. (Use **on the threshold**.)

435. Most road accidents happen in winter. And the average age of drivers involved in car accidents is eighteen. So, what are the two major causes of these accidents. (Use **a combination**.)

437. At twenty years of age, when he was half way through university, he left to go working as a driver. Ten years later, he wants a better job, so what does he **resume**?

439. Every one of his marriages was unsuccessful. Every relationship with a woman has ended in arguments and separation. He loves the company of women. But what has he **resigned** himself to?

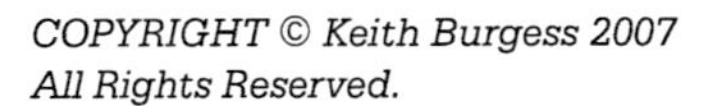

PART 3 Lesson 11: Superwords 401~440

Student B

Think through the vocabulary and increase your speaking skills by taking turns at asking and answering these questions.

Try to use the lesson words as you answer.

402. Asian food shops are **thriving** at the moment. Why? Wild cats in my area are **thriving**? Why?

404. He has been very violent and the police have warned him about his violence. His children are sometimes naughty. What does he have to **refrain from**?

406. His heroes are Eric Clapton, John Lennon and Eminem. He practises every moment on the guitar. What is his **aspiration**?

408. The opera singer was a great singer, but today his voice did not sound so great. What **hampered** his performance? It usually takes four days to sail from New Zealand to Australia. But this time it took six days. What **hampered** the progress?

410. Nations are usually firmly opposed to war. Yet Australia and Britain (and many other countries too) condoned the United States attack on Iraq. Why did they **condone** it?

412. South Africa set up its society like this, until the rest of the world said it **deplored** it. What actually did the rest of the world **deplore**?

414. My father always told me that using violence was wrong. But he was **hypocritical**. What actually did he do?

416. When karaoke became popular in Japan, what **proliferated** in every city?

418. He got a phone call soon after the job interview which made him feel **elated**? Why? What did they tell him? (Try to think of three things.)

420. Nobody wanted to share his flat, because it smelled so bad. Actually, he regularly cleaned his flat, but the cleaning was **superficial**. Can you explain?

422. If God visited us tomorrow, what would he say humans have **squandered**?

424. The family always makes sure their doors are locked and no windows are open at night. They have built a high fence around their property and have two guard dogs in their backyard. Why? What do they live **in** close **proximity to**?

Lesson 11: Student B

Superwords 401~440 continued...

426. He was only an average golfer. And he was playing by himself that day. But when he finished playing the course that day, he came away feeling very happy. Why? What had he **surpassed**?

428. In the middle of summer (or in Bangkok) what will make you feel **lethargic**?

430. What do bats **occupy**? What part of the Middle East did the United States **occupy** in 2004? What do young children **occupy** (so that parents never get any privacy or time to themselves)?

432. Their car broke down in the middle of nowhere. They were in trouble because they couldn't fix their car and they did not have a cell phone (and nobody knew where they were). Then, over the hill in the distance, they saw another car coming closer. What was **on the horizon**?

434. The majority of workers in the area worked in a mine which was a very dusty environment. The majority of these workers smoked. So, what was **prevalent** amongst the elderly workers?

436. It is **a myth** about cats, what is it? It is **a myth** about oysters, what is it? It is **a myth** about carrots, what is it? It is **a myth** about children, television and violence. What is it?

438. At thirty-four, in his medical check-up, it was revealed that he was very overweight and that he had a high blood-cholesterol level. So, what did the doctor **dictate**?

440. He had spent twenty years in prison when he did not commit the crime. The judge discovered this when new evidence was shown. How did the courts **rectify** this? The bank teller put $1,000 into the customer's account instead of $100. (He put the decimal point in the wrong place). How did he **rectify** this?

PART 3 Lesson 12: Superwords 441~480 Student A

Think through the vocabulary and increase your speaking skills by taking turns at asking and answering these questions.

Try to use the lesson words as you answer.

441. He was firmly against unemployed people receiving financial help, because he believed there were plenty of jobs. What did he **categorise** unemployed people **as**?

443. She loved swimming in the ocean. But that day she was **reluctant to**? Why?

445. My political science professor asked me to find out public opinion of the government's defence policy. I put together a questionnaire, interviewed over a thousand people, and tabulated the results. What was **thorough**?

447. Life has always been hard for the average worker in this country. But last year the cost of food went up 10%, the cost of rent 20%, and the average worker's wages went down 5%. What **deteriorated**?

449. What **gradually** happens to men but not usually to women, and it makes the men want to wear a hat?

451. All the customers thought that the gym was a bit old-fashioned. What needed to be **upgraded**?

453. His sister was a famous painter who exhibited her work at the best art galleries. He was very jealous of his sister's artistic talents. She wished that he was able to paint as well as her and that everybody admired him for his art too. And so, he did something **irrational**. What did he do?

455. He was fifty years old. He probably had fifteen more working years, which was not a lot of time. He wanted a better job or promotion, but his education was not high enough. What did he **contemplate** doing?

457. With the heavy rains, half of the farm was already flooded. Only his farmhouse and farm buildings on higher ground were safe. And then the river burst its banks. What **advanced**?

459. Although they love the countries where they were born and are leaving their families behind, people still choose to immigrate. Why? What are they **seeking**?

461. The company was so busy that the boss could not let his workers have a

Lesson 12: Student A

Superwords 441~480 continued...

holiday as he had promised. So, how did he **compensate**?

463. If man lands on the planet Mars one day and finds something **astonishing**, what might it be?

465. Their children had been at the high school for three or four years. It was in their neighbourhood and all their friends went there. When it was discovered that there was a drug problem in the school, the parents considered taking action but then decided it would be **an upheaval** for the children. What action did they think of taking?

467. The country, which has many lakes, generates its electricity mainly with dams. So, what is it **harnessing**?

469. Before gunpowder and guns, there were, of course, still wars but it was more difficult to kill the enemy with a spear or knife. Describe the wars after rifles were first made. (Use **subsequent**.)

471. My father always was very religious and proud of his honest behaviour. And then one day his wife (my mother) asked him if he loved her. And he did (for him) the **unthinkable**? What did he do?

473. He kept a lot of cash in the house and his wife had a fortune's worth of jewellery. He was very afraid that his house might be broken into and everything would be stolen. So, what did he **fortify** his house with?

475. My grandmother never travelled to another country, not even to a neighbouring country. In other words, what had she never gone **beyond**?

477. He weighed 105 kilograms and so he really wanted to lose weight. He began to exercise vigorously and was careful with how much food he ate. When he weighed himself again after two months he was 100 kgs. There was no **discernible** what?

479. In some societies the male child is much more important than the female, because the family expects to depend on the male to support the family later in life. Therefore, the male is often given more opportunities. Of course, the female can feel that this is unfair. What is one example of something she might **resent**?

PART 3 Lesson 12: Superwords 441~480

Student B

Think through the vocabulary and increase your speaking skills by taking turns at asking and answering these questions.

Try to use the lesson words as you answer.

442. Why do fashion models spend so much time in saunas and putting mud on their skin and being careful about their diet? (Use **preserve**.)

444. What is **severed** immediately after the birth of a child?

446. When her son graduated from university, she bought him a brand new car. What did this **exhibit**?

448. She was practising her singing by recording and listening to herself. She bought a new tape recorder but she was dissatisfied with it and so she returned it to the shop. Why was she dissatisfied? (Use **distort**.)

450. The school decided to change the school's hours so that students started studying at eight in the morning and finished at two. But this was too early for them. So, what did they tell the principal? (Use **existing**.)

452. For Christmas his auntie gave the brother and sister clothes store vouchers for $500 each. He was going for a job interview. She had just taken up surfing. So, what did they **select**?

454. The New Zealand dollar was losing its value against the value of the Australian and American dollars. So, the government took steps to **halt** what?

456. The doctor realised the businessman was a busy man, but he needed to take better care of his health. What three things did the doctor recommend about exercise, at midday and at least once a year? (Use **brief**.)

458. The lifetime of a human is conveniently divided by psychologists into three stages; **namely**, what?

460. He collected old-fashioned vintage cars and they were the most valuable things to him in the world. But when he needed a heart operation and he didn't have enough cash, what did he **resort to**?

462. Everyone loses a boyfriend or a girlfriend at least once in life. In your opinion, what is **the remedy** for a broken heart?

464. When the father was sentenced to prison for a terrible, terrible crime, the

Lesson 12: Student B
Superwords 441~480 continued...

media was not allowed to publish his name. Why not? And explain. (Use **for the sake of**.)

466. Inventions such as the automatic washing machine made life easier for people and saved their time. How? Explain. (Use **liberate**.)

468. When the teacher told the parents of the boy that their son had cheated in the exam, the parents said they wanted **tangible** proof. So, what did the teacher do?

470. The oldest living people in the world are said to be in Russia (not the United States or France or England). That seems **incredible**? Why does it seem **incredible**?

472. He has been a very successful entrepreneur. Years ago his income was merely $50,000 per annum. Now it is calculated to be $200,000. So, what has happened to his income? (Use **halve**, **double** or **quadruple**.)

474. We should make sure we do not pollute the rivers or streams. And we should limit the number of showers we have each day. Why? What is **precious**?

476. With our close friends and our family, we might talk about our feelings and our troubles. Or we might make important plans. But on the bus with fellow passengers or with our neighbours over the fence, we might talk about **trivial** matters. What are three **trivial** matters?

478. Should we do it **beforehand** or **afterwards**? a) Take out travel insurance. Go for a trip overseas. b) Put the cat outside the house. Leave home for work. c) Tidy up the house. Friends come around to visit. d) Stay with a friend for a week. Write a letter of thank you.

480. When the new highway was opened, there were five accidents on one bend in the highway in the first three hours. What was **urgent**?

PART 3 Lesson 13: Superwords 481~520

Student A

Think through the vocabulary and increase your speaking skills by taking turns at asking and answering these questions.

Try to use the lesson words as you answer.

481. She was going to marry the man whom she was in love with. But when she saw that he had terrible drinking habits and loved to gamble large sums of money, she changed her mind. Why? What did she **foresee**?

483. The television film crew followed the tornado. What did the pictures show that were taken **in the wake of** the tornado?

485. At the intersection there was **chaos**. Why?

487. **Absolutely** is often used with strong adjectives. For example, he was very clever – we say: "He was **absolutely** brilliant." What do we say for these? He was very, very cold. She was very, very pretty. He was very, very afraid.

489. After working for the company for only three months, the boss told the very ambitious worker something that **delighted** him. What was the news?

491. Street cleaning is a very low-paid job and people do not like to be seen doing this kind of work. **Thus**, what?

493. What happened **unexpectedly**? He did not take an umbrella to work, but when he arrived he was wet. He took a loan out from the bank to buy a new car. Then suddenly he was in financial trouble. Why? What **unexpectedly** happened?

495. He was always good at golf, but one day on the golf course he did something **remarkable**. What was it?

497. After cutting his leg with an axe, the forestry worker had to give up his job outside and go to work in the office. Why? (Use **irreparable**.) After an accident on the motorway, the taxi driver had to spend a lot of money. Why? (Use **irreparable**.)

499. What do brothers and sisters always **vie for**, especially in their younger years?

501. Going to the movies is an experience (compared with sitting at home watching a video). There is the wide screen, the people all around

Lesson 13:
Superwords 481~520 continued...

Student A

watching, the popcorn and soft drink, and often these days there are competitions for customers. What is going to the movies **altogether**?

503. The bicycle was not very popular with parents or children because the handlebars were wide and passing cars touched them. So, how did the company **modify** the bicycle?

505. Whenever you introduced her to a strange group of people, she always went red in the face. What was **visible**?

507. Although another company made him a good offer for a job, he decided to stay with his current company because he liked the people he worked with. What did he **resist**?

509. All the critics said he was the best actor in the movies that year. So, what did he **receive**?

511. When the woman complained of unfair treatment in the workplace (she had been overlooked for promotion), who **sympathised**? And how did they **sympathise**?

513. The members of the employers' organisation agreed not to offer pay increases to their workers that year. After it was announced, what was there **an epidemic** of?

515. Research has shown that some movies which deal with adult subjects are only suitable for children if there is an adult with the child (to talk with her or make sure she feels alright). **Accordingly**, what?

517. The bus driver travelled from Los Angeles to San Francisco, as he usually did on Mondays. There were no accidents on the road, none of his passengers got sick, and he left on time and he arrived on time. It was a **routine** what?

519. When she gets into the car and her children get into the back seat, she always looks to make sure the children have done up their seat belts. Why? What is she **mindful** that?

PART 3 Lesson 13: Superwords 481~520 **Student B**

Think through the vocabulary and increase your speaking skills by taking turns at asking and answering these questions.

Try to use the lesson words as you answer.

482. The department store was having a sale. The advertisement which they put in the newspaper had a misprint. Instead of saying 8% discount, it said 80% discount. When the shop opened at nine o'clock, what was it **overwhelmed with**?

484. There were three cinemas in town but most of the customers were going to the brand new one. Why? (Use **state-of-the-art**.)

486. She read her flatmate's diary. In the diary she read about her flatmate being in love with her boyfriend. But she knew that this boy was a rat. So, what was her **dilemma**?

488. Most people have to study hard to be successful at university. But she not only had to study hard, she also had to look after her family including her very sick mother. And when her husband ost his job, she had to take on a part-time job. So, throughout university, what did she have? (Use **extraordinary**.)

490. The honeymoon suite in a hotel is **exclusive** to who? There are seats in a theatre with an excellent view (called the balcony or box seats). Who are they usually **exclusive** to?

492. When you are signing a contract to pay off a new car, you should always read the small print on the document because what might it **mention**?

494. I don't want to be a teacher. The pay is too low. **Furthermore**, what?

496. Everything made him feel frightened. Preparing for exams, the first day of a job, or even asking a stranger for directions. And then he took a confidence-building course. What **evaporated**?

498. Some sports are easy to understand. Baseball, for example, in which you hit the ball and run. Or football, in which eleven people play against eleven other people to kick the ball into opposite nets. But how about cricket or American football? (Use **somewhat**.)

500. He is very, very strong. And he can get very, very angry. Sometimes he cannot control himself. Most people who know him fear him. Why? What do they think he is **capable of**?

Lesson 13:
Superwords 481~520 continued...

Student B

502. When the bank teller looked at the first customer coming in the door, what **alarmed** her?

504. The father gave his son the car for the night **on the condition that** what?

506. They say a champion chess player must have supreme concentration. So, what must a champion chess player be **oblivious to**?

508. His legs were badly damaged in the car accident, and at first he had to move around in a wheelchair. But he undertook therapy and strengthened his legs with exercises. What did he eventually **succeed in**?

510. The murderer was freed after ten years in prison. Then immediately he murdered again. When the judge sentenced the man for his second murder, he said he had **surrendered** a right. In fact, what right had he **surrendered**?

512. The vineyard was able to produce one hundred more cases of wine than they had the year before. Why? What was **abundant** that year?

514. He was a bus driver by day, but he spent all his evenings and weekend studying archaeology. Why? What was he **inquisitive** about?

516. Who **authorised** the bombing of Hiroshima and Nagasaki?

518. He got a job as a bodyguard to a famous Hollywood star. He was surprised to find out how hard she worked to make a movie and then promote it. What had he **envisaged**?

520. He went hunting in the bush for three weeks and then got lost for a long time. But he survived. When he came out his hair was down to his waist and his beard almost covered his face. What was he in **dire** need of?

PART 3 Lesson 14: Superwords 521~560

Student A

Think through the vocabulary and increase your speaking skills by taking turns at asking and answering these questions.

Try to use the lesson words as you answer.

521. She used to be a practising lawyer. Nowadays, all her time is taken up with looking after her young children and her home and garden. However, she still finds time to take a course which updates her on the latest changes in law. Why? What does she **intend to** do?

523. The chef quit his job because the boss kept **interfering in** the kitchen. What did the boss actually do?

525. Alcohol and supermarkets – what is **the issue**? Immigrants and unemployment – what is **the issue**?

527. He's lost in the forest. What is he **surrounded** by? The pop star has just left the concert hall and is getting into his car. What is he **surrounded** by?

529. The patient has just had a serious operation and has been returned to his room in the ward. What is being **monitored** now?

531. Teenagers suddenly become secretive and they value and demand privacy. For example, what do they **object to**?

533. If you are really in need of money and you find someone's wallet in the street (and nobody sees you), what does it **challenge**? It **challenges** your what?

535. When she was backing her car into a car park, her car lightly touched another car. The other driver asked for her name and address and sent her a bill for repair (for $500!). But she thought this was unfair? Why? (Use **microscopic**.)

537. The country put many troops and tanks along its northern border but not many along its other borders. Why? (Use **hostile**.)

539. The gardener thought that butterflies were destroying his tomato plants. So, what did he **examine**?

541. What is a **modest** house in your country? What is a **modest** income? What is a **modest** meal?

Lesson 14:

Superwords 521~560 continued...

Student A

543. They were listening to the radio that morning. So, they heard the information about the weather. They went out fishing and got caught in the storm. Three of them died. What did they not **take heed of**?

545. The road authorities **condemned** the bridge? Why? And what happened after they **condemned** the bridge?

547. If you are a guest, after the meal what are you **supposed to** do? In primary school, if the teacher asks a question and you want to give the answer, what are you **supposed to** do? If you accidentally run over a cat or a dog on the road, what are you **supposed to** do?

549. How many **decades** in one hundred years? For how many **decades** have you been alive?

551. 150,000 students entered university last year - about half were men and half were women. 40,000 males and 20,000 females graduated from university this year. **Statistically**, what?

553. A flatmate who is a musician and a flatmate who is a student are **incompatible**. Why?

555. She is studying to be a doctor, but she has discovered that she hates the sight of blood. She has tried and tried to overcome this reaction, but she cannot. So, what is **understandable**?

557. Because the atmosphere of the Earth is becoming more and more polluted, what is happening to the temperature of the Earth? (Use **increasingly**.)

559. He loved his girlfriend very much, and he thought that she loved him. But he was too shy to ask her to marry him. So, he proposed by writing a letter. But then he was **in agony**. Why?

PART 3 Lesson 14: Superwords 521~560

Student B

Think through the vocabulary and increase your speaking skills by taking turns at asking and answering these questions.

Try to use the lesson words as you answer.

522. She was experiencing hard times, being short of money and needing a job. Then by chance she met an old friend in the street. They chatted and the friend said she could perhaps get her a job and would call in a day or two. But she knew her friend's offer was not **genuine**? How did she know?

524. Some people smoke because they want their fingers to be busy or their mouths to be busy when they are relaxing or in a social situation. So, what could they do? (Use **substitute for**.)

526. At high schools, students can usually choose such subjects as accountancy, woodwork or the German language. But what is usually **compulsory**?

528. At home the father hit them and even beat them. In other words, what were his children **subjected to**? Also when he was unhappy, he said unkind things to his wife. In other words, what was she **subjected to**? Not only that, but at school the other children chased and hit these children. Or, in other words, at school what were these children **subjected to**?

530. Company products were disappearing and the boss suspected that the workers were stealing. So, the boss did something **drastic**. What was it?

532. When the hotel caught fire (even though there were firemen there), one of the guests rushed into the flames because he could hear a baby crying. Describe this guest using **on the part of**.

534. What is **the** best **climate** for growing grapes? What is **the** best **climate** for starting up a new adventure tourism business?

536. In the family there was mother, father, three children (7, 10 and 13) and one large dog. The father loved to spend his spare time cooking, while the mother liked to grow vegetables and herbs. They found an **ideal** house. Describe it.

538. A country that has been suffering war needs help. It is important that we send nutritious food as well as medical supplies there, because people who do not have good food are **susceptible to** what?

540. He was caught for speeding. He was travelling at 65 kilometres per hour

Lesson 14:

Superwords 521~560 continued...

Student B

in a 60 kilometre area. The policeman took down his details from his driving license. One week later he received a letter asking him to pay $500 for speeding. Where did he go? And what did he **query**?

542. Who is usually **the recipient** of the death penalty? Who can be the recipient of an Oscar? Not just the best or smartest students get scholarships to universities. Who else can be **a recipient**?

544. He could never get his son to be serious about his study. But his brother (who had a lot more money) was successful at getting his son to study hard. What method did his brother **employ**?

546. He found a wallet (which was empty) and took it to the police. The police immediately thought he was the thief. By accident, he took an important document home in his briefcase from work. He reported the accident the next day to his boss, who immediately fired him. What did he decide was **pointless**?

548. If a businessman wants to avoid paying tax, where does he **divert** his money?

550. A visitor to Singapore, which has strict environmental laws, was fined $500 and asked to leave the country. Why? What had he **discarded**? Where had he **discarded** it?

552. A working mother cannot look after her children, go to work, clean the house, help her children with their homework, take her children to ballet and sports clubs, do the washing and cook dinner for her husband's colleagues or clients. Why can't she? What is **finite**?

554. Alice and Frieda were twins. Alice was born at 11.55 p.m. on December 31, 1990. Frieda, on the other hand, was born at 12.02 a.m. on January 1, 1991. Today is December 31, 2000. So, despite being twins, today what are they **respectively**?

556. Movies which contain a lot of violence (even documentaries which are reporting violence that really happened) have age restrictions. Why is this so? (Use **immature**.)

558. The government has introduced a law which says that drivers cannot drive longer than ten hours a day. Who does this **have implications for** and why?

560. It is a fact that young teachers have **a** better **rapport** with students at high school? Why is this so?

PART 3 Lesson 15: Superwords 561~600 — Student A

Think through the vocabulary and increase your speaking skills by taking turns at asking and answering these questions.

Try to use the lesson words as you answer.

561. The daughter was good at language and history, but not so strong at maths and economics. The son, however, was talented at mathematics and economics, but found language and history very hard. So what did they do to improve this situation? (Use **and vice versa**.)

563. The government introduced a sex education course into high schools last year. This year statistics show that there were fewer unwanted babes born. So, **apparently**, what?

565. He loved his job, but always feared losing it. Then one day he won a million dollars in Lotto, so what did he **purchase**?

567. The parents loved their only daughter. So, they always told her they loved her, and they gave her everything she wanted and seldom pointed out her mistakes. But this was **detrimental**. How was it **detrimental**? And what was it **detrimental** to?

569. There have been a few cases recently of businessmen robbing themselves to get insurance. But the police are not worried. Why are they not worried? (Use **on a... scale**.)

571. Scientists say that it is impossible for anyone to travel across space between stars. But she saw with her own eyes a strange-looking spaceship travel across the sky at amazing speed, and then she saw it land in the middle of some fields. So, what is she **convinced that**?

573. On Monday, it was warm enough to go swimming. On Tuesday, you had to wear an overcoat if you wanted to go out. On Wednesday, he could take his shirt off when he worked outside. And on Thursday, he woke to find the frost had killed his tomato plants. Describe the situation for that week. (Use **a fluctuation**.)

575. The company claimed that it treated men and women equally. Yet when the salaries of men and women were compared, it was found that men on average earned far more than women despite their having similar jobs. Describe and explain the **discrepancy**?

577. She had never had a job when she had been studying at university. She never cleaned her room. Her garden was covered in long grass and weeds. Why? What did she **loathe**?

Lesson 15: Student A

Superwords 561~600 continued...

579. On the television news a street was shown in a rural town in America in which all the houses had **disintegrated**. Why? What had happened?

581. The pilot of the passenger plane forgot to fuel the plane before take off. **In effect**, what did he do?

583. She is a carpenter, what is **indispensable** to her? He is a priest, what is **indispensable** to him?

585. A photojournalist was caught in an explosion in Beirut. The car he was travelling in was completely destroyed and he was injured, but what, amazingly, was still **intact** and so he was able to carry on his job?

587. She had a very good income that year. She gained a promotion, her boss gave her an end of year bonus, she won money in Lotto and an aunt left her $50,000. So, she landscaped her garden, built an extra bedroom and bought new furniture. What did she **channel** her money into?

589. For a while there was quiet on the border between the two warring countries. What had **ceased**?

591. Only the pictures of the **elite** were on the walls of the International Sports Museum. Who were they, do you think?

593. The Chinese government gave regular warnings on television when the SARS epidemic occurred What did the warning **emphasise**, do you think?

595. The company says it is very proud of its record of treating men and women fairly. But, although they hire as many women as men, women are paid on average 10% less than the men. The company is **by no means** what?

597. For the first time in the country the people were allowed to express their feelings about the government, and newspapers were allowed to show pictures of the poverty, and editors were allowed to express their political opinions. What did the people suddenly **enjoy**?

599. If your city has heavy smog at night and you suffer from breathing difficulties, what is **unwise**? And what is **wise**?

PART 3 Lesson 15: Superwords 561~600

Student B

Think through the vocabulary and increase your speaking skills by taking turns at asking and answering these questions.

Try to use the lesson words as you answer.

562. One supermarket charges $1.50 for a half litre of milk. The other supermarket charges $2.25. One supermarket charges 75c for a newspaper. The other charges $1.10. There is a **marked** what?

564. He was a very **contented** cat? Why? (Give at least three reasons.)

566. The parents never taught the boy what is right and wrong. He almost never went to school but his school never told the parents. He was intelligent and succeeded in a course to become a plumber. But when he left the course, there were no jobs available. After all this, he became a criminal to make his living. Who does the blame **reside with**? And why?

568. The doctor carried out research on patients that had died of lung cancer. He found that only 10% of them had smoked all their lives. He found that 50% had never smoked in their lives but had partners who did. After this research, he was **satisfied** that what?

570. The language student did not live with native speakers. The only native speaker he spoke to regularly was the bus driver and he only said "hello" and "thank you". Thus, his speaking and listening skills did not improve. Finally, what did he decide to do? (Use **divorce**.)

572. The mother found out that when she said "well done" to her student daughter every time the girl had a good test result, the daughter worked even harder. And when she said "bad girl" every time a test result was bad, she gave up studying completely. So, what did the mother **suppress**?

574. The cafeteria at the Polytechnic employed trainee chefs. Some of them were excellent chefs and some of them were not. Some had had two years training and others just a few months. So, what was **erratic**?

576. When they tested the athletes for drugs at the Olympics the result of the test was negative. Yet, their performance was 100% better. Can you explain? (Use **minute**.)

578. When adopted children grow up who do they want to **locate**? How can they **locate** them?

580. The unemployment rate went up last year and so did the crime rate. Can you explain? (Use **accompany**.)

Lesson 15: Student A
Superwords 561~600 continued...

582. The buses were never on time and she often had to stand at the bus stop for a very long time. When two of the buses broke down on her route that day, what did it **prolong**?

584. The wanderer was crossing farm country when heavy rain began to fall. Where did he **shelter**?

586. All the young people planned to have an all night party, but he decided he couldn't join them. Why not? (Use **have commitments**.)

588. Although he had a lot of money and free time, and although he enjoyed meeting new cultures and seeing strange lands, he had never been abroad. Why not? What did he **fear**?

590. What **governs** the maximum speed of a car? What **governs** the speed of a truck? Can you think of at least three factors?

592. The council has a rule. Residents can make their fences out of any material but they must all be exactly two metres high. So, what must be **uniform**? He was a very good painter. The walls of the house were the same colour green all over. So, what was **uniform**?

594. The mother who lived next door to her offered to pay to look after her children at the same time that she looked after her own. The mother next door could then go back to work, and both would earn some money. But after two days, the woman at home decided she could not **cope**. Why?

596. He did not pass the entrance examination to go to the university. However, he was the best basketball player in the region, and the university wanted him as a player in its team. So, what did the university do? (Use **grant**.)

598. He was the first person in his family to ever go to university. So, when he checked the results board at the university and saw that he had passed his finals, what did he **immediately** do?

600. If you were looking down at China from the moon, what would be **prominent**? If you are looking at an ocean liner, what is **prominent**? If you are driving around the central district of Rome, what is **prominent**?

PART 3 Lesson 16: Superwords 601~640 Student A

Think through the vocabulary and increase your speaking skills by taking turns at asking and answering these questions.

Try to use the lesson words as you answer.

601. The champion football team won the competition every year for eight years. And then, what did they **suffer**?

603. The school teaches children how to look after their environment and how to keep their neighbourhoods clean. So, once a year they send the children into the streets around the school. What do the children **gather**?

605. Despite Israel being a very beautiful country with a lot of interesting history, not many tourists go there. Can you explain. (Use **volatile**.)

607. The country has many deep lakes which it keeps to generate electricity and for tourists to fish and enjoy water sports. However, the land has been very dry for a very long time and the farmers need water. So, what was the government's solution (to help the farmers but keep the lakes for electricity and tourism)? (Use **for the duration of**.)

609. The old lady could see the world in front of her, but nothing at all to the left or right or in the distance. She was **partially** what?

611. Most young people today have the complete freedom to choose what clothes they like to wear. And **likewise**, what?

613. In some countries, committing suicide is a crime, and people who survive suicide can go to jail. Some people are against this law. What is their main argument? Begin: "They believe that making suicide illegal...". (Use **deprive**.)

615. He was chosen by his country to represent it in basketball at the coming Olympic Games. He **declined**. Why, perhaps, did he **decline**?

617. He was a very popular doctor especially with young people. But the Medical Council decided to **suspend** his license. Why? And until when?

619. It was a very dry country, so farming was impossible. The scenery was poor, so no tourists came. Yet, it was a fabulously wealthy country. Can you explain? (Use **extract**.)

621. When travelling in buses, especially when they were crowded, he always kept his credit card in his front pocket. Why? What was he **wary of?**

Lesson 16: Student A

Superwords 601~640 continued...

623. In the United States approximately only 50% of the people take part in the national elections. Why, perhaps, is this so? (Use **disillusioned with**.)

625. She has a very tidy appearance. She keeps her house extremely clean. She loves fresh air and exercises regularly. A male colleague at work asked her out for a date, but she refused. Why? (Use **repulsive** and explain.)

627. The government had planned this year to provide every child under five years old with a free medical check up. But what **upset** this plan?

629. Coal fires and wood burners heavily pollute the atmosphere. **Conversely**, what?

631. Every time I saw my father he told me how easy it is to waste money these days, and how everybody needs to have money for unexpected events, such as losing one's job or the car needing expensive repairs. In other words, he **lectured** me on what?

633. Twenty years ago there were only three universities in the whole country. Twenty years ago the government did not offer loans to students to pay for their education. Describe this situation using a right and **a privilege**.

635. The forest was part of a national park and many hikers walked in it. However, there were also deer there, and hunters also illegally used the park. When the hiker heard a gunshot, what did he **instinctively** do? (And it saved his life.)

637. In this country there is wealth for everyone, and every parent believes that children need to be loved, looked after, treasured, and protected. So, in third world countries, what do these parents think is **obscene**?

639. Can you name four things found in every home that could be **lethal** to a child?

PART 3 Lesson 16: Superwords 601~640

Student B

Think through the vocabulary and increase your speaking skills by taking turns at asking and answering these questions.

Try to use the lesson words as you answer.

602. Which pictures are usually most **graphic** – ones found in family photo albums, on television, in the newspaper, or at art galleries? What are the pictures usually of – picnics, sports events, war, the scenery, or public meetings?

604. The tourism board wants to **promote** this country as a great tourist destination. What is the best way to do this?

606. Why are the trains in Japan called bullet trains? (Use **a fraction**.)

608. The Council wants to widen the roads and take some land from property owners to do so. A court must decide whether this can be done or how much money the Council must pay. Who should make up the court? Who would be **neutral**? The mayor? Property developers? Transport operators such as bus companies? Citizens from a neighbouring city? Members of the central government? Choose and explain.

610. He is forty years old and has never worked. His parents are very wealthy. He has studied at universities (higher and higher) all of his life so far. He wants to be chosen to be a government member in the coming elections. But he is not very popular. Why not? (Use **appreciate**.)

612. I passed my exams but it was a **marginal** pass. What score do you think I got (50% is a pass)?

614. This country exports a great many trees for not a great deal of profit. In the countries that import these trees, the trees are made into furniture and houses. The companies that do this make huge profits. So, **logically**, what should this country do?

616. This morning on the bus she noticed that her blouse buttons were not done up and neither were her shoe laces. Why? (Use **hastily**.)

618. If you are feeling very tired after a full day's work, there are usually two ways of **reviving** yourself. Can you name them?

620. You were told by a neighbour that, according to the news, there was an escaped murderer seen in your part of the city. How would you **verify** this?

622. He was born and bred a Scotsman. How was it **conspicuous**? She was born in India and belonged to the Hindu religion. How was it **conspicuous**?

Lesson 16: Student B

Superwords 601~640 continued...

624. He didn't care about not being rich and he didn't care about not having a loving wife because, at eighty-five, what was he **blessed with**?

626. All his sons and daughters came to visit and pray for him. Why? What was **imminent**?

628. He didn't even take a raincoat when he went cross-country walking. Before the foreign student went to university, she had not taken an academic reading and writing course. She was told that the library opened at eight-thirty in the morning, but when she got there she saw a sign that read "Open each day at 10 a.m." Use **ill-** to describe these people.

630. Fast food chain stores like McDonalds exist mainly to make profits. What do they also **fund**?

632. He used to welcome friends and family to his house. But then he won a million dollars and everyone wants their share. So what he does **shun** now?

634. The country had computers, but instead of being the small size they are today, they were the size of wardrobes or refrigerators. And the country had improved communications, but three telephones in three houses had to share the same number. What was **primitive**?

636. The public schools and the private schools both run computer classes, but the private school has one computer for every child, while the students in the public school have to share. Likewise, at sports practice, there is a football for very player at the private schools, but one whole team has just two balls at the public school. Why? (Use **a disparity**.)

638. Even though the people are decent and honest at heart, there is more petty crime in the poorer section of the community. Can you explain? (Use **sheer**.)

640. Liberal thinkers want the courts to give the children of divorcing couples equally to the mothers and the fathers. That is, they want the judges to make sure the fathers have the children in 50% of cases. Other people, are in favour of **the status quo**. What is **the status quo**?

PART 3 Lesson 17: Superwords 641~680

Student A

Think through the vocabulary and increase your speaking skills by taking turns at asking and answering these questions.

Try to use the lesson words as you answer.

641. The Council has put cycle lanes on the sides of every road in the city to make cycling safe. But cycling in the city is still very dangerous. Why? (Use **inhale** to explain.)

643. Today there are a lot of wealthy people with spare money who do not know where the best place is to invest it. So, what is a **lucrative** job nowadays?

645. The American President regards The British Prime Minister as an excellent statesman, and so too does the Prime Minister regard the President as an excellent statesman. So, what is **mutual**?

647. Three men whom she liked very much asked her, at different times, to marry her, but she refused. Her friends arranged blind dates, and her parents invited promising young men around to meet her, but, although she was attracted to many of them, these meetings never came to anything. Why? What was she **determined to** do or **determined to** be?

649. These used to be **commonplace** in homes fifty years ago before the invention of PCs (personal computers). What were they?

651. If you are studying for a Science degree at university, what subjects does Science embrace? If you are studying for an Arts degree, what subjects does Arts embrace? If you are studying in the Humanities, what subjects does it **embrace**?

653. They went out together for seven years as girlfriend and boyfriend, but then they both found other partners. So, what never **eventuated**? What is predicted (especially by religions) at the end of every century, but so far has never **eventuated**?

655. New cars became too expensive for the average worker when the local car assembly factories closed. So, what was there **an influx** of?

657. Farmers in Western countries are usually more **prosperous** than farms in Asia, especially in countries like Thailand or Japan. Why is this so?

659. He argued that teenagers should not be given sex education at high school because, if they did not know about sex, they could not get into trouble. But this argument was **flawed**. Explain.

Lesson 17:
Superwords 641~680 continued...

Student A

661. A teacher can give his students this when he has only six students, but he cannot when he has forty. He does not have the time. What is it? "He cannot give his students... ". (Use **individual**.)

663. Some people say mathematics is easy. Some people say mathematics is hard. Can you explain? (Use **subjective**.)

665. Every ambulance driver and paramedic finds the first six months of work very difficult. But then it becomes easier as they get more experienced. What, in fact, do they become **conditioned to**?

667. He sold his house, left the woman whom he did not love, quit his job of twenty years, and spent all his savings on a three week trip around the world. He then found himself alone, penniless, and wondering about his future. Why? What had he **erroneously** believed?

669. He broke the world record for the 1000 metre race. What did he **excel at**? She won best film at the Cannes Film Festival. What did she **excel at**?

671. The government won a lot of public support when it showed pictures of a neighbouring country's military build up and promised to increase the size of the armed forces. What did the government **manipulate**?

673. He had been a lawyer for many years and won 90% of his cases in court. Why? What did he **have a** good **command of**?

675. When people buy pets, they often forget that their pets can live a long time – cats for over ten years and dogs for over fifteen years. So, they sometimes abandon them. Why do they **abandon** them? And where do they **abandon** them?

677. In his latest letter to his mother he did not mention his girlfriend once. But he usually wrote about everything he and his girlfriend did. What did the mother **infer**?

679. He did not separate from his wife, but he had a girlfriend outside of his marriage for years. Describe this situation. (Use **ongoing**.)

PART 3 Lesson 17: Superwords 641~680 Student B

Think through the vocabulary and increase your speaking skills by taking turns at asking and answering these questions.

Try to use the lesson words as you answer.

642. She and her boyfriend have been planning to get married for two years. The wedding is in two weeks, and she is always talking with her friends about whether she really wants to marry or whether he is really the best person for her. What **phase** is she going through?

644. When flight was first invented by man, people dreamed of international travel. But what took decades to **materialise**?

646. He was travelling from New York to Chicago by plane and from Chicago to St Louis by train, and wanted to get there as soon as possible (i.e. not lose any time at all). So, what did he have to **coordinate**?

648. She wants to take time off work to do a course and still be paid. Who will have to **approve**? Why will he **approve** or **not approve**?

650. Some people say that unemployed people are lazy, but at certain times in the economic cycle what are **non-existent**?

652. She got the job of head chef because she said she had worked in this position before. This was true, but she only had the job for two days while the head chef was away. So, in her new job of head chef what **surfaced** soon?

654. She was a very keen reader as a child. In fact, by the time that she was five years old, she was reading five books a week, **albeit** what?

656. Describe these people using **solitary**. He was the only person travelling on the bus that day. There was no other person crossing the national park that day. She had one-on-one lessons with the teacher.

658. In his country, eighteen-year-old boys go into the army for a year, which is a very tough life. He is seventeen. So, what does he **dread**?

660. Suddenly, in the 1960s, most people could sit at home and both listen to and watch the news of the world. With **the introduction** of what?

662. My mother won't let me help her clean her house (although she is really too old for such work). She won't let me even give her a ride in my car to the shops. She prefers to take herself by bus. In fact, she will be angry with me if I try to help her in any way. (Use **fiercely** to describe her.)

Lesson 17: Student B

Superwords 641~680 continued...

664. To stop shoplifting, the shop owner put surveillance cameras at the entrance and the exits. Why was this **ineffective**?

666. Name three **minor** sports in your country. Name three **major** ones. Name three **minor** illnesses. Name three **major** ones.

668. What usually **precedes** marriage? What usually **precedes** divorce? What **preceded** DVDs? What usually **precedes** an industrial strike?

670. The wealthy man walked up to the beggar on the street and generously handed him a check for $20,000, which was enough to start a new life. Years later, the beggar was able to **reciprocate**. What happened?

672. When Mount Everest was successfully climbed in 1953, how did the world hear about it so quickly (the climbers were still climbing down)? (Use **relay**.)

674. Can you name one issue which is likely to **polarise** people? Explain your reason.

676. What is the usual ratio of students and teachers in high schools in your country? What is **the** likely **ratio** of policemen and the public in this or in your country?

678. What **hierarchy** do you usually find in a high school?

680. She did not like clubs, and she was not the kind of person who enjoyed meetings or belonging to organisations, but when she decided (like many other people) that she did not like government policies, she became active. (Use **participate in** to describe her action.)

PART 3 Lesson 18: Superwords 681~720

Student A

Think through the vocabulary and increase your speaking skills by taking turns at asking and answering these questions.

Try to use the lesson words as you answer.

681. Not everyone believes that physical punishment is wrong. Not everyone believes suicide is wrong. But most members of society have the same **core** values. What are they, do you think?

683. The twins looked exactly alike, yet for everybody they were **distinct**. How, do you think?

685. The police had witnesses that saw the man breaking into the house. They found a lot of stolen property in the man's flat. Yet there were no fingerprints belonging to the man anywhere in the house. What did the police **deduce**?

687. The university needs 500 fee-paying foreign students each year. So, they take the top 500 students in the IELTS or TOEFL examinations. In this situation, what is **arbitrary**, and why can it be described as **arbitrary**?

689. One hundred years ago women did not have the right to vote. Now there are at least three heads of countries who are women. What has **progressed**?

691. He is a very tough judge. He sentenced a rapist, a man who accidentally killed a child on the road with his car, and an elderly man who assisted his sick and dying wife to die, all to life imprisonment. What did the judge **equate** all these crime **with**?

693. Which two of these do you expect to be **rigid**? Say which two and explain your choices. A golf club? The bumper of a car? The working hours of a teacher who teaches when other teachers are sick? An airline company's timetable? A policeman's attitude to speeding drivers?

695. Say which one of these were or are **concurrent** and explain why the others are not: The lives of Winston Churchill and Adolph Hitler. Breakfast and lunch at McDonalds. Recovering in hospital and having an accident. Working part-time and studying part-time.

697. He ran away from fighting in the war, was caught and court-marshaled. Thereafter, what was he **labelled**?

Lesson 18: Student A

Superwords 681~720 continued...

699. Everyone talked about the **so-called** army. Why did they say **so-called**? Everyone talked about the **so-called** hospital. Why did they say **so-called**?

701. She was the only child in the family and had always lived with her mother and father in a big house. When she went to live at a boarding school in a dormitory, what did she have to **adapt to**?

703. They say we are **orientated towards** different people at different times in our lives. Who are we **orientated towards** at these ages and why do you say so? A two-month-old baby. A seven-year- old boy. A teenage girl. A young man or woman at twenty-five. A seventy-year-old.

705. The soldier fell to the ground and lay **passive**. He was not dead and he was not injured. So, why did he lie down **passive**?

707. He worked as a marriage guidance counsellor for many years. What did he **have insights into**? She worked as a private secretary to the Prime Minister. What did she **have insights into**?

709. At what precise moment does a baby become **an entity**?

711. All the other boys were bold enough to invite girls out. But he wasn't. What **inhibited** him?

713. He was a very ambitious young man. At work he made sure that the boss heard about his successes and about his colleagues failures. What was his **agenda**?

715. What is **the sequence** for using a bank card at an ATM (Automatic Teller Machine)?

717. He was going on a three week overseas trip. He was going to go through five Asian countries in that time. And then he heard that the airline pilots were on strike and refusing to land in China. So, what did he **revise**?

719. Who usually **articulates** the concerns of the workers to the bosses?

PART 3 Lesson 18: Superwords 681~720

Student B

Think through the vocabulary and increase your speaking skills by taking turns at asking and answering these questions.

Try to use the lesson words as you answer.

682. In this country it is illegal for parents to hit children, but how can this be **enforced**?

684. In this country, because there are so many elderly people, not everyone receives a pension when they retire at sixty-five. Who does the government **differentiate between**?

686. Not enough people were using the bus after ten o'clock, so what did the transport company do? (Use **terminate**.)

688. After two hours of counting votes at the general elections, the authorities could not say for sure who had won the election, but they had a strong idea who was going to win. So, what did these authorities give to the media? (Use **preliminary**.)

690. Having your own business gives a person a lot of self-control and usually a better income. But what **offsets** this?

692. Trains used to be the most common form of transport across Europe. What **displaced** them?

694. The rules of the road are **straightforward** at intersections where there are no traffic lights, aren't they? What are they?

696. All imported cars in this country cost approximately the same amount. Yet far more Japanese cars are driven on the roads than others. What is there **a bias** against? And why, do you think?

698. In the small town there was a family of tradespeople – a carpenter, a plumber and an electrician. When the plumber repaired the pipes in houses, he always made sure there was still a leak from one of the hidden pipes. Why? What was his **motive**?

700. He did not have to travel far or even cross the road to buy his weekly groceries. Why not? (Use **adjacent to**.)

702. His torch would not work but it was not broken. So what did he do? (Use **insert**.)

Lesson 18: Student B

Superwords 681~720 continued...

704. He lost a thousand dollars at the casino in one night. But he still went back the next night. Why? What did he want to **recover**?

706. She was probably the most intelligent student in the class, but in the examination she only came fifth. So, what is there **scope** for?

708. When his wife gave birth to their first child, he bought cigars for all his male colleagues. Why? What did he want to **communicate**? When he heard that an old school friend's wife had died. He sent flowers. Why? What did he want to **communicate**?

710. He wanted to buy a house, so he went to a bank which was offering a **flexible** house loan. What kind of loan was the bank in fact offering?

712. Before a football match begins, what do the officials **inspect**? Why? Before the US invaded the country, what did United Nations officials go into Iraq to **inspect**? At five o'clock the soldiers in the army camp get up and their sergeant **inspects** them. What does he **inspect** and why?

714. It is a high school which teaches the usual range of classes (including maths, science, language). The students are being trained to have music careers. They also are taught to play the piano and orchestral instruments such as violins and to sing. So, what is **integral** to the school's programme and why?

716. Her plan was to get a degree in medicine within three years, but she **deviated from** it. How? What did she do actually?

718. He arrived at the airport just before seven o'clock, but had to wait three hours for his plane to arrive because he had been given **misinformation**. What was the **misinformation**?

720. Why is there always **an interval** between applying for a travel visa and getting one? Why is there always **an interval** between getting pregnant and finding out that you are pregnant?

PART 3 Lesson 19: Superwords 721~760

Student A

Think through the vocabulary and increase your speaking skills by taking turns at asking and answering these questions.

Try to use the lesson words as you answer.

721. The government reduced taxed by 10% that year to improve the income of its people. But what **negated** it?

723. Where do private schools get their **revenue**? Where do public schools get theirs?

725. A policeman was caught accepting money from a member of the public to not give him a traffic fine. The authorities thought that this might be happening a lot. So, what did the police force **undergo**?

727. What **triggered** the landslide?

729. He was always a top tennis player, but this season he became the best tennis player in the world and especially good at delivering aces. Why? What did he **refine**?

731. More cars come into the City Centre now. So the volume of what has increased? The electricity department was able to produce more electricity this year from its dams. Why? **The volume** of what was greater?

733. When he was a young man, he was a soldier. He thought they were the best years of his life. He enjoyed getting up at five, the hard work and the discipline. Now, years later, he finds himself in prison after getting caught for a serious crime. But he doesn't mind. Why not? (Use **reminiscent of**.)

735. Every country is represented at the Olympic Games. Outside the stadiums what do you see **an array** of (which decorates them)?

737. Buses, taxis and airplanes are **modes** of what? Telephones, faxes, and email are **modes** of what? Shops, mail-out catalogues and television infomercials (ads) are **modes** of what?

739. He was from Latvia and he was studying in an English language school. There were a lot of friendly students and the school had translation of important information in most languages, but he felt **alienated** there. Why?

741. His own parents taught him the art of telling lies; his older sister taught him how to cheat at school; and he saw his grandparents steal milk from neighbours' letterboxes. What did he have no **notion** of?

Lesson 19: Student A

Superwords 721~760 continued...

743. The daughter told her parents that she should be sent to university overseas and not her brother (or both of them), because she had done much better in examinations than him. This was a **potent** what?

745. In the tale of The Tortoise and the Hare, who **overtook** who and why? The cinema used to be the most popular entertainment medium, but what **overtook** it?

747. The mother measured her daughter at six years old and found her height was one metre zero point two. She measured her again at the age of seven and found she was one metre zero point three. What was **incremental**?

749. The bank offered her a second bank card with $1,000 low interest credit. But she **hesitated**. Why? And what did she finally do (and why)?

751. The twenty-four-hour shop could not survive. Why not? What was **alongside** it?

753. This was her first time to Australia and she found a job there. She could not get a work visa to start her job for three weeks but had some money in the bank. So, what did she do **in the interim**?

755. If you get colds easily, what is **advisable**? If you have been married three times and each marriage ended in divorce, what is **advisable**?

757. When you change your address, who should you notify? If a doctor tends to a patient who has come to him with a shotgun injury, who should he **notify**?

759. The cat had kittens, so what was **the gender** of the cat?

PART 3 Lesson 19: Superwords 721~760

Student B

Think through the vocabulary and increase your speaking skills by taking turns at asking and answering these questions.

Try to use the lesson words as you answer.

722. She had very **liberal** views regarding abortion. What were they? She also had **liberal** views regarding violence being shown on television. What were they?

724. How do employers **supplement** staff when they suddenly become really busy?

726. In some countries the governments actually run and own the newspapers, television and radio. Why? (Use **vehicle**.)

728. My two favourite television programmes are on different channels. I can watch the whole of one programme but only half of the other one. Can you explain? (Use **overlap**.)

730. I was talking with a friend about a movie I had seen. He saw it when he was on holiday in Europe. I saw it here. He thought the acting was really good. I thought it was poor. We usually have similar tastes and make similar judgements. Can you explain? (Use **a version**.)

732. He had no bad habits but sometimes he needed a pick-me-up. So, what did he occasionally do after work at the bar? (Use **indulge in**.)

734. Inflation is down. Business confidence is up. Statistics show that unemployment is down to its lowest level in decades. The standard of living is at its highest in decades. So what is **burgeoning**?

736. The investor made a lot of money when the value of the Japanese Yen suddenly went up, but other investors did not. How was this possible? What did the investor have? I asked my client to meet me at 7 o'clock at a restaurant but he could not make it. Why not? Why could he not meet me? What did he have? (Use **prior**.)

738. My car was in a road accident but I decided not to repair it. Instead I made a claim to my insurance company and bought a new one. Why did I choose to do this? (Use **extensive**.)

740. What are three **desolate** places on this Earth. Which is the most **desolate**? Give your reason.

Lesson 19: Student B
Superwords 721~760 continued...

742. Entering a new boyfriend or girlfriend relationship. Bungy jumping. Being accepted by a top university. Driving a car over 200 kilometres per hour on the open road. Which, in your opinion, is the most **thrilling**? Again, give your reason.

744. He was a very religious man (he had strict rules for himself for doing right and not wrong). But when he lost his job and he could not support his family, what was he **tempted to** do?

746. At the party, the man asked her a question and from the question, she thought that he was interested in her as a possible girlfriend. But it was just an **innocent** question. What was the question, do you think?

748. He was third in the first 2000 metre running race at the Olympics. So, what did he **qualify for**?

750. Statistics show that ten years ago 2,000 people died each year from lung cancer. And five years ago 4,000 people died from lung cancer. What do you think will be the statistic this year, and describe the situation. (Use **exponential**.)

752. He was afraid of making promises. And he was afraid of long-term relationships. So what did he never **venture to** do?

754. She was a top scientist who had won awards in her field. She had also represented her country at international sport. In addition, she worked for charities and had helped found a children's hospital. But she was also a very modest person. So, what did she **downplay**? And what, perhaps, did she in fact say?

756. He was only a worker, but he made most of the decisions in the company. So, what was he **virtually**?

758. The indoor stadium was not big enough for most sports events (it had seats for up to five thousand spectators). And the town had no place to show movies. So, what did the stadium also **function** as?

760. It is very dangerous for pilots to fly in mountainous areas when there is fog and snow together. Why? (Use **confuse with**.)

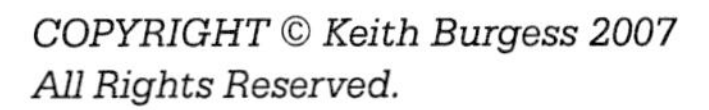

PART 3 Lesson 20: Superwords 761~800

Student A

Think through the vocabulary and increase your speaking skills by taking turns at asking and answering these questions.

Try to use the lesson words as you answer.

761. The house removalists had to **dismantle** the piano. Why?

763. When he finished high school he had two choices - go on to further education or get a job. Who gave him **guidance**? And what was **the guidance**?

765. Unfortunately, some students at primary school are **ridiculed** by the other students. Who are they?

767. Hundreds of climbers have tried to climb Mount Everest, but what **frustrated** them? Terrorists often try to board airplanes to take control of it, but, fortunately, what **frustrates** them?

769. When he saw the little boy, he suddenly thought that he was possibly the boy's father. Why did he think this? What did he **glimpse** in the boy?

771. When East Germany broke away from West Germany after the Second World War, what did the East German government **construct** and where?

773. The politician worked very long hours on government policy to improve the economy. Unfortunately, his marriage broke up because of this. But the politician did not regret this. Why not? What did he believe? (Use **subservient to**.)

775. By blowing up bombs in or near public facilities, what are terrorists aiming to do? (Use **inflict on**.)

777. The water supply of the industrial city became undrinkable. Why? (Use **deposit**.)

779. When the family visited the popular tourist resort, it was the peak tourism time. They had not booked, and in the end they had to sleep in tents at the camping ground. Why? (Use **vacant**.)

781. They say that certain developing countries will never be economically free of Western countries. Why not? (Use **the magnitude**.)

783. When the boss travelled overseas on holiday, he expected the sales in his supermarket would decrease without him there to drive the staff. But, actually, sales increased. What did the boss **underestimate**?

Lesson 20:

Student A

Superwords 761~800 continued...

785. He was living in a foreign country as an ambassador to that country. When he was caught drink driving, he drove away at speed to his government's buildings. After that, the police could not arrest him or punish him. Why not? (Use **immune**.)

787. Who do seven-year-old boys **worship**? Who do young soccer players **worship**? Who do nuns **worship**?

789. For years the husband had a drinking problem and, when he got drunk, his behaviour was rough and unkind. What **ultimatum** did the wife give her husband?

791. Their marriage did not seem secure **from the outset**? Why? What happened?

793. He **fared** very **well** in the exam? What happened exactly? The new magazine, that was published for the first time last week, **fared** very **well**. What happened?

795. After ten years of teaching, most teachers get tired and worn down and don't care so much for their students, but he was different. What happened? (Use **remain**.)

797. All she did was forget her husband's birthday, which was easy to do. But the husband thought this was **significant**. Why did he think this?

799. When teenage boys reach the age of eighteen, it is quite a dangerous age **insofar as** what?

PART 3 Lesson 20: Superwords 761~800

Student B

Think through the vocabulary and increase your speaking skills by taking turns at asking and answering these questions.

Try to use the lesson words as you answer.

762. He **supports** his elderly parents (who don't have a pension). How? She **supports** the political party at election time that promises to reduce crime. How? He **supports** the Greenpeace Organisation (which looks after the environment). How?

764. All of the children at the school, except one small boy, were sad and upset when their teacher died. They could not understand how such a terrible thing could happen. Why was the small boy not sad or upset like the others? (Use **experience**.)

766. Use "**Presumably**, ..." to answer these questions. Why are so many people carrying umbrellas this morning? Why isn't Fred wearing a wedding ring anymore? Why has the cost of bread suddenly increased?

768. The parents could buy a house (which they have always wanted, but never had), but instead they use the money to provide their child with a good education. What does it **testify**?

770. The couple both had very good jobs with good incomes. But their children needed to be looked after when they both were not at home. And their employers expected them to dress very well. So, what was **eroded**? And how?

772. What can ambulance drivers **legally** do when they have to get to an accident soon?

774. The wife is dissatisfied with the amount of housework her husband does. But she now has an absolutely fair system. She has drawn up a list of jobs which need to be done each week around the house **whereby** what?

776. She hated being the teacher's favourite student for always being right, so what did she **deliberately** do? These customers were always complaining unfairly about the quality of the food or the cooking, so what did the chef **deliberately** do?

778. Economic times were not good. She was an honest person who discovered that the chemist she worked for was selling drugs to teenagers. But she was not **outspoken**. Why not?

Lesson 20: Student B

Superwords 761~800 continued...

780. Answer using **travel**. He got caught and fined when he was driving in a restricted speed zone? Why? The city has very reliable and comfortable buses, but they are almost always empty. Why?

782. When he was out walking in the country one morning, he saw a hill and decided to climb it. But he got lost because it got dark before he reached the top. Why? What was **deceptive**?

784. It is natural that children **take** their parents **for granted**. Why should they be thankful? Their parents have always been there. Look around you now. In our modern technological world, what do <u>we</u> **take for granted**?

786. You think the novelist is **promising**? Why do you say so?

788. Unlike other mothers, the mother did not give her children any pocket money without them doing jobs around the house first. Why? What did she **reason**?

790. In the World Cup football final, the referee stopped the game and gave a player a red card, sending him off. This **bewildered** the player? Why?

792. If a bank robber with a gun orders the bank staff to give him money, should they **cooperate**? Why or why not?

794. This was her first marriage and she was twenty-five. This was his third marriage and he already had five children. What was she **enthusiastic** to do, and what was he not **enthusiastic** to do? Why and why not?

796. The criminal had been to court so many times before that he knew the justice system very well. And he had a good understanding of his case and the evidence. So, what did he **dispense** with?

798. What is **the mission** of firemen? What is **the mission** of soccer coaches? What is **the mission** of a lifeguard at the beach?

800. He had to work much harder and there was a lot of stress when he got the promotion. The money was good, but it was **at the expense of** what? Also, he never got to see his children's graduation ceremony and he forgot his wedding anniversary. Yes, the money was good, but it was also **at the expense of** what?

PART 3 Lesson 21: Superwords 801~840 **Student A**

Think through the vocabulary and increase your speaking skills by taking turns at asking and answering these questions.

Try to use the lesson words as you answer.

801. What are Russian men **notorious** for? What is Mexico **notorious** for (especially for American couples who are unhappy with each other)? What was President Clinton **notorious** for?

803. What are the **mainstream** subjects at university these days? In your country what are the **mainstream** opinions on homosexuality? On abortion? On prostitution?

805. In this country, suicide is illegal. In this country, personal freedom is regarded as very important. Is this **a contradiction**? Discuss.

807. Young boys like loud music. In their cars they always have their CD players turned up loud. In fact, they have four speakers – two for the front and two for the back of the car. Why? (Use **engulf**.)

809. A young child, unfortunately, was run over in the street. She was only six years old and she was playing there. The driver was breaking the speed limit at the time. It happened on the corner of a road where sixteen such accidents had happened before. Three years ago the Council said they would improve the road condition. In your opinion, who is most **accountable** and why? And how could they be held **accountable**?

811. The gifted medical researcher had been researching cancer for years when suddenly he died of a heart attack. This was terrible. Why? (Use **on the brink of**.)

813. When spies are caught, they never want to reveal their secrets. But they can be **coerced**. How? Reading is not a popular pastime for young people these days. But they need to read to succeed at school. How can they be **coerced**?

815. A marriage was arranged for him by his parents. They chose his partner. But he married the girl he was truly in love with. So, this was **contrary to** what?

817. Car accidents at speeds of fifty kilometres per hour are seldom **fatal** in modern cars. Why not? She left her two-year-old child playing near the river for only two minutes, and this was **fatal**. How?

Lesson 21:
Superwords 801~840 continued...

Student A

819. On average it takes young men who have graduated from business college and entered a company five years to reach middle management. On the other hand, it takes women with the same background on average eight years. What **accelerates** the young men's promotion?

821. The grandparents lived nearby in a two-bedroom appartment. The rent for a four-bedroom house was getting too high for the family of four to afford, but they had to live somewhere. Who **proposed** what? And what was the children's reaction?

823. The taxi-driver had fifty-five customers three weeks ago, thirty-five customers last week, and twenty customers this week. So, what is **diminishing**?

825. The owner of a company should never keep files related to finance on the main computer which all the staff use. Why not? (Use **commercially**.)

827. In the 1970s computers suddenly became cheap enough for the average household to own. So, what was there **a boom** in?

829. The government has spent millions warning people about the dangers of smoking. **Yet**, what?

831. The hotel clerk was in the room alone with all the visitors' bags. How could the hotel clerk benefit if he was dishonest? (Use **an opportunity**.)

833. Israel was becoming a popular tourist destination, and then war broke out there again. What was the result? (Use **dramatic**.)

835. Today is the day that students choose and enrol in their university courses. Teaching is not a very financially rewarding job. **Even so**, what?

837. The State of Hawaii has its own unique identity and a strong economy. What is more, it is quite some distance from the United States. It is surprising, then, that Hawaii has not **declared** what?

839. The tenant in the rented apartment is always late paying the rent. In addition, he is always holding loud parties, although the landlord has forbidden it. What is more, the tenant has damaged the property. This is **grounds for** what?

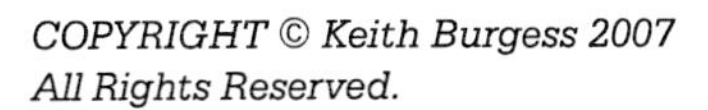

PART 3 Lesson 21: Superwords 801~840

Student B

Think through the vocabulary and increase your speaking skills by taking turns at asking and answering these questions.

Try to use the lesson words as you answer.

802. What do open windows and a lot of uncollected daily newspapers outside a house **attract**? Why?

804. He was an extremely wealthy businessman. Yet, he was **envious of** many of his less wealthy friends. Why? Can you explain? When they are interviewed, who do popular film stars say they are **envious of**?

806. A woman was lost in the desert with her two children. One child was surviving well but the other was quite sickly. She was absolutely sure that she had just enough water for them all for a week. But she knew there was no help and they had a two week walk. So, she had to be **ruthless**. What exactly did she do?

808. In which Olympic event do runners need **the** most **stamina**?

810. The man bought a very cheap stereo which was advertised in the newspaper. And then the policemen visited him and took it away. Why? What had he **unwittingly** done?

812. Most of the writing on ancient vases is **unintelligible** for two reasons. What are these reasons?

814. There were always queues at the village library, because their methods of giving out books were **antiquated**. What were their methods?

816. The police warned the neighbourhood that a burglar had been breaking into many homes in the area. His neighbours were not **complacent**. What did they do? What happened to them? He was **complacent**. What didn't he do? What happened to him?

818. The speeding driver was finally caught when he arrived outside the hospital to drop off his dangerously ill son. The policeman arrested him and took away his car. This was **unwarranted** for two reasons. What were the two reasons? And perhaps what was **warranted**?

820. What did Adolph Hitler want to **dominate**? Brazil has for a long time had a champion football team. What does it **dominate**? The government owns and operates most businesses in the country. What does it **dominate**? Whenever she was with a group of people, she did most of the talking. What did she **dominate**?

Lesson 21:
Superwords 801~840 continued...

Student B

822. After his father died, he took three months off work and went to a lonely spot in the country. There he spent all his time, sitting in a chair in the garden or walking amongst nature. Why? What was he **pondering**?

824. What do schoolchildren usually put in their schoolbags to take to school? (Use **along with**.) What should you pack for an emergency when you go on a camping holiday? (Again, use **along with**.) What are the three best forms of exercise? (Once more, use **along with**.)

826. In many large factories there is a loud siren that sounds at eight in the morning and then again at five o'clock in the late afternoon. What does it **signal**? When he went out with girls, he usually wore casual clothes and took them to the movies or bowling. With this girl, he wore his most stylish clothes and took her to an expensive restaurant. What did it **signal**?

828. The fruit on display in the fruit basket in the lounge looked juicy and fresh, but actually it was **inedible**? Why?

830. In his opinion, you are alone in the world and the rest of the world wants to beat you. It is what **versus** what? Either you can have a narrow and low-lying car that travels at 200 kilometres per hour, or a wide one that you can move around in. But you cannot have both. It is what **versus** what?

832. When the football player was kicked by an opposing player who did he **appeal to**? To do what? When she failed her final exam by only 1%, who did she **appeal to**? And for what, or to do what?

834. In the hospital the doctors decided to **isolate** the patient? Why?

836. When the soldier, who was serving overseas, got a letter from home telling him his father was very sick, what did he **request**?

838. When the Australian dollar **strengthened** against the American dollar, was this good news or bad news for importers in Australia? Explain.

840. The cheese-making factory which supplied every supermarket in this city **expanded** its market? How?

PART 3 Lesson 22: Superwords 841~880 **Student A**

Think through the vocabulary and increase your speaking skills by taking turns at asking and answering these questions.

Try to use the lesson words as you answer.

841. She had a terrible, terrible time. She became widowed and unemployed at the same time. So, what **coincided with** what?

843. This winter absenteeism at work and at schools has increased by 50%. Why? What has **struck** the population?

845. What **relieves** stress, although you should not have too much of it?

847. There is a vast difference between learning English to become a receptionist in an international company and learning English to be an interpreter. What is the **vast** difference?

849. At football matches fans supporting one team may become very violent against the fans who support the other team. Why does this happen? What or who do the fans **perceive** the other fans **as**?

851. Why do air crashes seem to be **unavoidable**? Why is paying school fees for children **unavoidable**? Why are failures in exams **unavoidable**?

853. Can you complete these statements?

If you are a window cleaner on the outside of the thirteenth floor of a building, you should take **extreme** ____________ .

If you are in the deep water with a shark, you are in **extreme** ____________ .

Even living on the second floor makes him very nervous. He has an **extreme** ____________ of heights.

855. The busy couple who both had careers moved out of a three bedroom suburban house with a garden into a one bedroom upstairs apartment. Why? To **lessen** what?

857. In a typical family, most of the income is spent on food, rent and clothing. How about the **remaining** income?

859. How do you **quantify** production in a factory that manufactures cars? How do you **quantify** safety in the workplace? How can you **quantify** love in a family?

Lesson 22:
Superwords 841~880 continued...

Student A

861. How do you **evaluate** the economic success (or failure) of a government?

863. The country has a lot of farmland but the economy depends mainly on tourism. Why? (Use **much of**.)

865. At university what do art subjects **cover**? What do social science subjects **cover**? What do economic subjects **cover**?

867. In this country, the cost of living is high in areas to which goods have to be transported long distances. But **elsewhere** the cost of living is quite low? Where is **elsewhere**?

869. There is something you can decide to do if you don't want any more children. But it is **irrevocable**? What is it?

871. He is seventeen years and two months old, while she has just turned eighteen years old. What is **comparable**? He earns $55,000 a year and she earns $62,000 a year. What is **comparable**?

873. He picked his new girlfriend up for the date fifteen minutes late. What did this **convey**? He wore jeans and a T-shirt to the job interview. What did this **convey**?

875. In most countries tobacco companies are not allowed to advertise smoking using famous actors. Why not? What does such advertising **depict** smoking **as**?

877. There were thirty-seven passengers already on the bus. There were six people waiting at the bus stop. The bus driver stopped but only let three more people on the bus. Why? (Use **maximum**.)

879. These days you can pay fifty dollars for a new washing machine, take it home and then pay ten dollars a week for about two years. Most people don't want to use this method to buy a new car. Why not? (Use **sizeable**.)

PART 3 Lesson 22: Superwords 841~880

Student B

Think through the vocabulary and increase your speaking skills by taking turns at asking and answering these questions.

Try to use the lesson words as you answer.

842. When the cost of timber and bricks went up substantially, what was there **an escalation** in?

844. Why did the teacher **confiscate** the student's cell phone? Why did the policeman **confiscate** the man's fishing rod? Why did the librarian **confiscate** the woman's library card?

846. The government put up the price of petrol. What did it **discourage** people from doing? How can the government **discourage** people from having too many pets?

848. Businessmen have to socialise and drink a lot. In fact, it becomes part of their daily life. So, what problem do they often not **recognize**?

850. When I went to dine out with my children, there were several restaurants I could have eaten in. I had a look first at the restaurant called "The Family Inn" and chose that one. Why did I choose this one? (Use **offer**.)

852. What does every national soccer team **desire**?

854. When children are failing at school, what do teachers do that is **counterproductive**? And what do parents do that is **counterproductive**?

856. The youngest brother had a million dollars in the bank. The oldest brother had a million dollars in the bank too. But only the youngest brother can be considered **affluent**. Can you explain?

858. Why are spicy foods so common throughout Asia? (Use **associated with**.)

860. Increased incomes mean people have money to spend on leisure and entertainment. **Hence** what?

862. The government has announced that new immigrants can send their children to school for free, and that immigrants over sixty-five can get an old age pension like the local residents can. How did the local people react? (Use **protest**.)

864. The husband is a gifted artist and the wife is a talented story teller. So, what did they **collaborate** to do?

Lesson 22:
Superwords 841~880 continued...

Student B

866. In a lot of research on pets and elderly people, it has been found that people with pets live longer and suffer from less mental illness than people without them. So, what is **well-documented**?

868. The pop band has just recorded its first CD. A major record company is going to promote and distribute it throughout the United States. The reviews in the music magazines are saying it is a wonderful CD. What is the pop band **on the point of**?

870. What does cosmetic plastic surgery **alter**?

872. He is married and he has school age children. His boss can offer him promotion in the company if he is willing to move to another city. His wife says no. Why? What does moving to another city **entail**?

874. The brother and sister had very different lifestyles but both were workaholics. Twenty-four hours a day, seven days a week, fifty-two weeks of the year she spent looking after her children. He did the same with his career. Describe them. (Use **devote**.)

876. At the end of a hard day's work all she could do was lie on the sofa and watch television, although there was a meal to cook for her son and the house needed cleaning. Why? What was **depleted**?

878. He was a brilliant lecturer, but the students, who were expected to take notes, complained because he spoke too fast. So, the university had to replace him. Why? (Use **keep pace with**.)

880. The father saw some bargains in a clothes shop. He bought some trousers and some shirts for his son and daughter. But when he got home, he found none of the clothes actually fitted them Why not? (Use **gauge**.)

PART 3 Lesson 23: Superwords 881~920 **Student A**

Think through the vocabulary and increase your speaking skills by taking turns at asking and answering these questions.

Try to use the lesson words as you answer.

881. 90% of the population pay their taxes to the government on time. Why is this so? (Use **otherwise**.)

883. The twentieth century was a troubled century. But there was **a period** of peace. When was it?

885. New parents should not be surprised at how much work babies are. Why not? (Use **the nature.**)

887. What do you need to have to be fresh and clean every day? (Use **daily**.) Organisations need to have this fifty-two times a year to keep in touch with their members. (Use **weekly**.)

889. The government wants sprinkler systems (which automatically spread water when temperatures get very hot inside) to be put on the ceiling of every building in the country. And then what will be **preventable**?

891. What is **a** necessary **component** of the security of a country?

893. What was she **optimistic** about? She held a party immediately after the exams. She did not bother hiring a lawyer to defend her in the court case. She did not take out health insurance when she went on a trip overseas.

895. She really wanted to become a lawyer. But she was a single parent and she felt her children needed her at home. But instead of becoming a lawyer, she spent ten years raising her children and then she felt it was too late to become a lawyer. So, what did she **sacrifice** and for what?

897. He got malaria and then was back on his feet and at work in a few weeks. (Describe what happened using **rapid**.) He started out in the company as a messenger boy, but very soon he was a middle manager. (Again, describe what happened using **rapid**.)

899. The earthquake caused landslides which blocked the tranport system into the city. So, what had to be done? Complete this sentence: "They used a ____________ to **remove** ____________ from ____________ ."

901. The government increased taxation on tobacco, but it has not reduced the quantity of cigarettes being smoked. What do you think this **indicates**?

Lesson 23:
Superwords 881~920 continued...

Student A

903. Complete these two sentences. "A shop reducing the price of its products will **generate** more ____________ . But it probably will not **generate** more ____________ ."

905. She ordered a hairdryer from a catalogue for $20. But when the parcel arrived, the bill inside was for $25. Why? What did the price in the catalogue **exclude**? Who do private schools, of course, **exclude**?

907. Any woman in the world can marry any man in the world from any culture. But what **tends to** happen? A strong-willed person who loves the smell and taste, and whose body needs the chemical, can succeed in giving up smoking. But what **tends to** happen?

909. He was excited to enter medical school and he was very talented and able, but he never studied hard. So, what did he not **realise**? He loved flying, but when he applied to join the Flying School they discovered that he was short-sighted. So, what did he never **realise**?

911. Can you name four news media? (The newspaper, etc.) In your opinion, which of the four media reports the news best and the second best? (Use **rank** and give your reasons.)

913. The rice fields had no rain for three months. **Consequently** what? The suburb was very near the City Centre and had wonderful facilities. **Consequently** what?

915. My brother loves soccer. **To what extent** does he love soccer, do you think? I don't trust my flatmate. **To what extent** do I not trust my flatmate, do you think? My girlfriend's father does not allow her to be independent. He's very protective. **To what extent** is he like that, do you think?

917. He spoke Mandarin Chinese fluently. When he visited China, the first person he spoke to could not understand him at all. Why not? And what was his **misconception**?

919. Who do parks, beaches and the streets **belong to**? Who does the future **belong to**? Who has the responsibility to keep this planet clean and green? (Make sure you use **belong to**.)

PART 3 Lesson 23: Superwords 881~920

Student B

Think through the vocabulary and increase your speaking skills by taking turns at asking and answering these questions.

Try to use the lesson words as you answer.

882. A man's cousin was awarded the Nobel Prize. Even though he did not help him in his work and he was only a distant relative, this man could still feel what? (Use **a degree**.) Likewise, another cousin was caught shoplifting. He did not help in the crime and he was only a distant relative. Still, he felt what? (Again, use **a degree**.)

884. "Dinosaurs and the white Indian tiger are two creatures that have become extinct." Add two statements to this using **the former** and **the latter**.

886. Complete this statement: "It is easy to significantly reduce crime. **Leaving aside** ____________ , in my opinion, all criminals who offend more than once can be put in prison for a long time."

888. Who do local manufacturers **compete with**? What do new graduates **compete for**? The car sales company gives a bonus each year for their most successful salesman. Who do these salesmen **compete with**? What do supermarkets **compete for**?

890. Some schools will still physically punish students. Parents are keen to send their children to these schools. Why? What do the parents **subscribe to**?

892. Students from poor families who are the first to go to university will work much harder than students from wealthy families to earn scholarships to universities. Why? (Use **represent**.)

894. Michael Jackson was his hero and so he **emulated** him? How did he do this?

896. Some patients who go into Accidents and Emergency at a hospital have to have operations and some do not. Why? (Use **differ**.)

898. What to do about household rubbish is a worldwide problem. In my city, the residents recycle glass, plastic, metal and paper. **Thereby** what?

900. Leaving food on the floor and not cleaning cupboards, and having holes in the floors of houses **invites** what?

902. The couple really loved each other. And they both wanted to have children.

Lesson 23: Student B

Superwords 881~920 continued...

Unfortunately, the husband was infertile. They had two choices (or perhaps three). What were they? Which did they choose to do? (Use "**Rather than**...".)

904. What **determines** the price of a second hand car? Think of at least four factors.

906. Statistics prove that businessmen are more likely to have heart attacks than people who work in other kinds of employment. It is true that businessmen have less chance for exercise than other workers. But what is the **underlying** cause?

908. In Western culture what are two **appropriate** question to ask when you are first introduced to someone? What are two **inappropriate** questions?

910. If a drunk driver kills someone in an accident, and the police take his license away and then he drives without a driving license and he kills another person, what does this **justify**?

912. To be able to borrow money from the bank, what is **essential**? To be a successful singer, what is **essential**? The young man asked permission from his girlfriend's parents to marry her. What did the parents say was **essential** first?

914. Despite scientific advances, the fact that no cure has been found for the common cold **is largely due to** what? What was mass unemployment amongst office workers in the 1970s **largely due to**?

916. In a mature person, what are three or more **factors** that influence health?

918. She never worked in her life, yet she was never poor. Can you explain it? He was the only one in the family who had not **inherited** a big build and black hair from his parents. Can you explain? (Use **inherit**.)

920. Businesses that provide staff when there are sudden staff shortages can always be sure their businesses will do quite well. Why? What happens to any staff member **periodically**?

PART 3 Lesson 24: Superwords 921~960

Student A

Think through the vocabulary and increase your speaking skills by taking turns at asking and answering these questions.

Try to use the lesson words as you answer.

921. The South of France is a popular holiday destination these days. So, if a person in the street there has an Asian face, what do the local people **assume**?

923. For years scientists have been sending messages out into space in the hope that there will be a reply. If or when there is a reply, what will it prove? (Use **the existence** or **exist**.)

925. Governments around the world have promised to significantly reduce ozone-depleting gas emissions from factories. But environmentalists are **sceptical** about this. Why?

927. He was a trained carpenter, a trained teacher and a trained business manager. What did he have? (Use **a diversity**.) In parliament, besides Europeans, there are women from Japanese, Tongan and Egyptian backgrounds, as well as men with Korean, Canadian and Chilean backgrounds. What could we say about the parliament? (Use **a diversity**.)

929. Forensic scientists found the husband's fingerprints on the weapon that killed his wife. Also, blood spots on his shirt in the laundry were proven to be his. So, what did the scientists **establish**?

931. If mankind does not start looking after the Earth's environment better, what will **ultimately** happen? If a university awards degrees too easily, what will **ultimately** happen?

933. Honestly, where do you think the solution for poverty **lies**?

935. The couple did not have much of a social life until they found a reliable babysitter. How did this change their lives? (Use **enable to**.) He loves movies and watches them again and again on DVD. Now he's bought himself a second DVD recorder. It is very useful. How? (Again use **enable to**.)

937. He doesn't always arrive at work on time, but he works quite hard. So, **basically** what is he? A typical Japanese apartment does not have much space, but there is a kitchen, a lounge and a bedroom and a little bit of privacy. So, **basically** what is it?

Lesson 24: Student A

Superwords 921~960 continued...

939. If a student at university is sick for two or three months in his final year of his degree, the university will still sometimes award him a degree, **provided that** what? (Think of two **provisos**.)

941. He went for a three-day trip into the forest. He could work out directions from the stars. So, he did not take a compass. But he still got lost. What did he not **take into account**?

943. He was an honest, decent and law-abiding bartender, but he served a fifteen-year-old boy alcohol. Why? What did the boy **claim**?

945. Although she and her husband were not happy for many years, she still kept her positive spirit and good sense of humour. So, what did she **survive**? Inflation was suddenly high. Businesses everywhere were closing from financial difficulty. But still the government was elected again. So, what did the government **survive**?

947. The husband did not come home until two o'clock in the morning. But **at least** he did what?

949. Students from the private school did much better in the state exams than the students in the public schools. How were they **advantaged**? People from African countries have less success in the Winter Olympic Games than people from Scandinavian countries. How are they **disadvantaged**?

951. What was Sir Edmund Hillary the first to **accomplish** in 1953? What was Neil Armstrong the first to **accomplish** in 1969? What were the Wright Brothers the first to **accomplish** in 1903?

953. It makes sense that men work and women stay at home **given that** what? It seems unlikely that there are such things as ghosts **given that** what? It is not wise to go night after night to the casino **given that** what?

955. The boss offered a 5% wage increase. The workers had a meeting about it. What were **the** two possible **outcomes**?

957. The clean environment makes this country enjoyable. But the lack of entertainment makes it quite a dull place. (Use **–ly,** ...**-wise** to describe this country.)

959. To the following situations, add **a time phrase** that suits the time: Young people are getting married later in life. With the terrorists attacks on London and New York City, the world seems to have become more dangerous. Scientists are saying that there will be only one sex.

PART 3 Lesson 24: Superwords 921~960 **Student B**

Think through the vocabulary and increase your speaking skills by taking turns at asking and answering these questions.

Try to use the lesson words as you answer.

922. It is difficult sometimes to get airline tickets, **specifically** when? Some countries are much more multicultural than others, **specifically** where? My overseas friend asked if he could stay with me and I said "yes". I told him **specifically** how long he could stay. What actually did I say to him?

924. Two teenagers kidnapped a young boy and asked the boy's parents for money to return him. The teenagers were caught and put on trial. The judge's sentence was very **controversial**. What was the sentence? Why was it **controversial**?

926. The government put a series of advertisements on TV showing the terrible injuries that result from drink-driving. Who did it **have an impact on**? And in what way did it **have an impact**?

928. His income: full-time job $35,000 a year. Rent from a flat he owns (but does not live in) $10,000 a year. Where does he get his income from? (Use **in part**.)

930. It is said that money is better spent on poverty than on space exploration because people are dying right now. Say you believe this too. (Use **compelling**.)

932. If you add spice to a bland dish, what will it **enhance**? If an athlete takes certain drugs immediately before a race, what will it **enhance**?

934. *(You can use your dictionary to answer these questions.)* What is the wonder drug Aspirin **derived from**? What is penicillin **derived from**? What can starch be **derived from**? A man is afraid of flying or even climbing a ladder or using an elevator. Can you explain the fear? (Use **derive from**.)

936. Imagine: the governments of the world unite and pledge to introduce and enforce one-couple, one-child policies to solve the overpopulation problem. What is your prediction? (Use **surely**.)

938. What do you expect a motel to **provide**? At break-time when you are working for a company, what do you expect the company to **provide**?

940. The neighbourhood to the north of mine has a busy airport with airplanes roaring in and out all day, while the neighbourhood to the South is populated mainly by elderly retired people who seldom leave their houses.

Lesson 24: Student B
Superwords 921~960 continued...

My neighbourhood has some busy roads and people of various ages. Describe my neighbourhood. (Use **relatively**.)

942. He's a wealthy man. So, he goes for a holiday anywhere he wants, **regardless of** what? He's a teacher and he loves his job. It makes him feel very fulfilled and he just loves doing it. So, he would work there forever, **regardless of** what?

944. Her father owned a huge taxi company. When she graduated from university, she went to work for him. He wanted her to know the business well. So, in the company, what did she do **initially**?

946. It would be great if work environments such as factories were completely safe. But, unfortunately, there will always be **a certain number** of what? And why is this so?

948. There are a few clouds on the horizon. But they are not very dark and they appear to be going away. So, what is there **a** slight **prospect** of?

950. She felt she did not have any energy. So, instead of taking walks or swimming for exercise, she just stayed at home. How did it **exacerbate** the problem?

952. The City Council says there are too many incidences of dogs attacking dogs in suburban areas. What should the council do? (Use **restrict**.) Too many car accidents happen with young drivers after dark. What should the government do? (Use **restrict**.)

954. The road was wet and he had not had much sleep. Speed was the cause of the accident but what were **the contributors**? In the ancient city almost all of the buildings fell down in the earthquake. The earthquake caused the buildings to fall, but what was **the contributor**?

956. The government, which believes that the people cannot be wealthy unless businesses are successful, collects enough tax, but there is never enough for hospitals or schools. Can you explain why? (Use **concentrate on**.)

958. Two criminals were sentenced for the same crime. One received five years in prison and the other received ten years in prison. Why was one criminal sent to prison for ten years? (Use **previously**.)

960. You put washing on the line after not doing so for a week. What annoying thing **invariably** happens? When you pay a lot of money for a product, what do you **invariably** see in a shop the next day?

PART 3 Lesson 25: Superwords 961~1001 **Student A**

Think through the vocabulary and increase your speaking skills by taking turns at asking and answering these questions.

Try to use the lesson words as you answer.

961. Western economies are looking for alternative forms of energy such as wind and solar power. Why? What have these economies **exploited**? Policemen can never go on strike. Why not? Who would **exploit** this situation and how? (Use **exploit**.)

963. Her husband makes all the money but she can buy whatever she likes. What **has** she **access to**?

965. His company was bankrupt and so he had no money to pay his creditors whom he owed varying amounts. However, his warehouse still contained many unsold products which legally he could not sell. He felt guilty and really wanted to pay his creditors. So, what did he do? (Use **equivalent**.)

967. A friend used to smoke a lot and then gave up. Then he took up drinking and became an alcoholic. So, he took up jogging and now can't stop himself doing it. What does this **suggest** about him?

969. **According to** whom? An extremely big earthquake is going to hit California in the United States within the next twenty years. The Russians are placing weapons along the Russian-Afghanistan border. Maradona used his arm to beat the English football team at the World Cup.

971. She is a fashion model because she loves clothes. But she is also very shy by nature. So, which **aspect** of her job does she not like? Her husband is a professional golfer. She wants to know that there is a regular income coming in. So, which **aspect** of her husband's job does she not like?

973. If a worker chooses to work for one company for a long time, what is this usually **directly related to**? And what, therefore, is this **indirectly related to**?

975. Students could save a great deal of money if they choose to have two beds in each room and to share the bedroom. Although, **obviously**, what? Manufacturers could have much higher quality products if they used first-class raw materials. Although, **obviously**, what?

977. Why is it wise to register mail if you are sending something valuable through the post? To **ensure** what? ("To **ensure** that, if... .")

979. What **sector** does he work in? He cleans offices at night. He works as an ambulance driver. He slaughters sheep and cows at the meatworks. He

Lesson 25: Student A

Superwords 961~1001 continued...

tutors in mathematics. He delivers packages and parcels around town. He's a diplomat for his country in the Embassy in Beijing.

981. The townsfolk just stay at home in the evenings drinking beer. Why? What is the town **devoid of**? He could never be a famous actor or even be chosen to act in a local play. Why? What is he **devoid of**?

983. What is **inevitable** or will **inevitably** happen in these situations? A new husband leaves his young wife at home alone a lot. The police are going to stop their random check for drunk drivers. The new law bans shops selling cigarettes to underage people. But there are not enough police to enforce it.

985. Whether we should try to save endangered species is **questionable**. Some people say this. Why? What are they thinking?

987. The policeman signalled to the driver of the car to stop and the car took 500 metres to come to a stop. Now make a statement using "**Clearly,** ... .". There is a dairy, a clothes shop and a bakery in my neighbourhood and all three of them have announced that they are closing. "**Clearly,** ... .".

989. He did some research and found that if he bought the building products now and paid for a builder's labour now, he would have to pay $100,000 to build his house today. So, what had he **assessed**? The baker bought a sample of flour from one producer, a sample of flour from another, and baked two cakes with the same recipe. What was he **assessing** exactly?

991. She is a doctor and a specialist in her field. Her brother only works in a laboratory. She is **considerably** what?

993. He cannot give up smoking because he does not **possess** what? He never knows the time, because he does not **possess** what? Every business which he has started has gone bankrupt? Why?

995. Can you make a comment about these situations using **entire**? He's an addicted gambler. He goes to the casino at about 7 p.m. and does not leave until it is morning. All nations must agree to get rid of nuclear weapons. Or else what might happen?

997. She is an English language student from Sweden. She is at a party. Her English language is not yet strong, so she is quiet. She is concentrating; listening to what people are saying to understand and learn. The other guests know none of this information. What is their **perception** perhaps?

999. What is **negligible**? She buys her food at any supermarket she happens to be passing. Why? The voting public is very apathetic this year. Only 50% of the population voted in this year's election. Why didn't they care? What was **negligible**?

PART 3 Lesson 25: Superwords 961~1001

Student B

Think through the vocabulary and increase your speaking skills by taking turns at asking and answering these questions.

Try to use the lesson words as you answer.

962. Perhaps one day everybody will speak English as if it is their mother tongue. If so, this will be a **universal** what? Everybody should be allowed to criticise their own government. This is a **universal** what? And can you name three **universal** problems?

964. Girls and boys need to socialise with each other and learn how to get along with each other. But some people say the advantages of single sex schools **outweigh** the disadvantages. How?

966. The government no longer provides free education at university level, and, in fact, it has been found that 40% of people who enter university do not graduate. What does this fact **demonstrate**?

968. In the former Soviet Union (Russia), if a citizen was **critical of** the government, what happened? In a game of football, if a player is **critical of** the referee, what can happen?

970. He had a strong fear of flying. But he made himself fly because he was a businessman and flying around the country was necessary. When he was on board and the plane was in flight, his fear was too great and he did something **irrational**. What did he do?

972. In the first three weeks the Council's new recycling scheme collected 4,500 tonnes of recyclable materials from households. What does it **appear**?

974. The government put up the tax on imported goods. Who **benefits from** this? How do they **benefit**? There is a bus strike this morning in the city. Who will **benefit from** it and how will they **benefit**?

976. The foreign student wanted to stay in the country another six months. So, what did she have to **extend**? The editor told the journalist that he did not have to hand in the report on Friday after all. Sunday night would be OK. So what did the editor **extend**?

978. They say if this planet gets too crowded, we could live on other planets in another solar system. But this is not **feasible** yet, is it? Why isn't it **feasible**?

980. Can you use **noticeable** or **noticeably** for these situations? Your friend's

Lesson 25: Student B

Superwords 961~1001 continued...

clothes all look too small on him. Your friend used to drive the newest Porsche. Now he drives a second hand Toyota.

982. What are these speakers **implying**? "You spend a lot of time relaxing in the lounge and watching TV." "Those clothes are very tight on you now." "It is known that the pilot of the crashed aircraft had had personal problems recently."

984. His landlord put up the rent by $50 a week. How did he **respond**? Her father promised to buy his daughter a car if she could graduate with honours from university. How did she **respond**?

986. What did they **proceed** to do? The bakers returned from their morning tea break. Through the oven window, they could see all the bread was finished being baked. The Civil Defence Organisation received a tsunami warning. So, what did it **proceed** to do?

988. Her pet bird died in its cage. Why did this happen? What did she **frequently** do? The TV repair shop decided to give the customer 10% discount? Why? What did the customer **frequently** do?

990. The course is getting harder and she's failing all her tests. What **stage** has she **reached**? He is always complaining when with his friends. He never has anything cheerful to say. What **stage** has it **reached**?

992. Student visas can be renewed again and again. So, "**Theoretically**, what?" It takes nine months for a woman to gestate or have a baby. So, ... "**Theoretically**, what?"

994. Does your country have a strong, well-equipped, and large armed force i.e. army, navy and/or air force? What should be the role of your country's armed forces, do you think? (Use **primarily**.)

996. Use **predominantly** to answer these questions. Who supports young people at university? Where do most university students earn money?

998. There are only two realistic ways that an owner of a company can afford to **maintain** staff levels during a period of lower than usual sales. What are they?

1000. When a young man becomes a soldier, he usually has to stay in the army for five years but sometimes he is **released**. When?

1001. Many parents urge their children to study hard and to go to university rather than join the workforce as soon as they are able to leave school. Why? What are the parents **aware of** or **that**?

DEMONSTRATION EXERCISE CORRECTIONS

Corrections to exercise answers on pages 25 and 26:

page 25:

Q1. *...~~am~~ not aware that New Zealand is good for studying English.*

...was not aware that New Zealand is (or "was") good (or "a good place") for studying English (or "to study English").

Q2. *...was not aware that this country is so cold in winter.* [correct]

or "...was not aware that this country was so cold in winter."

Q3. *At first time in IELTS class it was very difficult ~~to~~ me because I was not aware of ^ difficulties of this class*

At first my IELTS class was very difficult for me because I was not aware of the difficulties of this class.

page 26:

999. *There will be negligible waste that you will notice.*

There will be negligible waste. (The meaning of negligible includes "that you will notice.")

1000. *...so that he ^ release the anger which he felt toward his father.*

...so that he could release the anger which he felt toward (or "towards") his father.

ACADEMIC WORD TEST - ANSWERS

1A
a. warn
b. a great deal
c. deteriorate
d. become aware
e. courageous
f. plan
g. timetable
h. shorten
i. improve
j. excitement
l. whole

1B
l. collect
m. own
n. vow
o. build
p. environment
q. let down
r. event
s. share
t. unbroken
u. at first
v. popularity

2
a. precisely
b. advocate
c. inform
d. eventually
e. correct

3A
a. find
b. count
c. bring/take
d. start

3B
a. (i) find (ii) discovered
b. (i) deliver (ii) brought
c. (i) initiate (ii) starts
d. (i) count (ii) calculate

Please note:
The suggested answers to the digitalised versions of the Academic Word Test — on the CD-ROM and also available online as a *FREE TEST DOWNLOAD* — differ slightly due to the type of question format.

4A
a. preservation
b. selection
c. fortification
d. construction
e. resentment
f. upgrading

4B
a. Selection of the right candidate...
b. (The) preservation of the historical documents...
c. (The) fortification of the city...
d. (The) upgrading of public transport...
e. Resentment of siblings...
f. (The) construction of the Pyramids...

4C
a. microscopically
b. modestly
c. ideally
d. drastically
e. genuinely
f. immaturely

4D
a. He behaves immaturely.
b. The house is ideally situated.
c. The government has drastically changed the tax laws.
d. I think he is genuinely sorry.
e. The computer programmers were modestly paid.
f. The paintings were microscopically drawn.

5A
a. extraordinary – progress / gift
b. exclusive – school / restaurant

c. irreparable – damage / harm
d. abundant – resources / supply

5B a. It was an exclusive restaurant.
b. It was an abundant supply.
c. It was extraordinary progress.
d. It was irreparable harm.

6A a. Life is ephemeral.
b. University education should be available.
c. Young people like to get married in historical buildings.
d. Statistics can be complex.

6B a. Typically, ...
b. Admittedly, ...
c. Historically, ...
d. Surprisingly, ...

6C a. as well as
b. the extent of
c. as is the case with

7 a. The parliament is in control nationally.
b. The city is in control locally.
c. No country or body is in control globally.
d. The provincial government is in control regionally.

8A a. employment
b. transportation
c. waste

8B a

9A a. proportion
b. proportionate
c. disproportionate
d. disproportionately

9B a. The number of part-time male workers is disproportionately high.
b. The number of child deaths is disproportionately low.

10A a. I underestimated the cost of the trip.
b. Apparently, tonnes of dust are deposited from outer space on the Earth each year.
c. The area was vacant for years because the land was too expensive.

10b a. ...all planets...
b. ...they are too immature to drive.
c. ...maths and science.
d. ...the increase in the prices of wine.
e. ...it is small and under threat.
f. ...keeping his staff.

10C a. The fact that people are more concerned about making money and have trust in science, accounts for religion and going to church being so much less popular these days.
b. A basketball player hitting another player in a game justifies him being expelled from the game.
c. Couples choosing to have such small families these days is largely due to the huge cost of raising and educating children.
d. It testifies to how much the parents value education, and that they regard the children as their future.
e. Paying for childcare, and spending money on entertaining clients, eroded their income.
f. Ambulance drivers can legally break the speed limit and ignore red lights.

LEXICON

LESSON 1:

1 the performance
2 meanwhile
3 generally
4 influence
5 achieve
6 a correlation
7 conclude
8 acquainted with
9 practically
10 an incidence
11 comparatively
12 attribute to
13 identical
14 particularly
15 consume
16 in other respects
17 with regard to
18 contain
19 integrate into
20 vital
21 account for
22 threaten
23 prompt to
24 principally
25 ignore
26 a decline
27 several
28 require
29 witness
30 reverse
31 allocate
32 originally
33 the consequence
34 favourable
35 permit to
36 accommodate
37 surplus
38 substantial
39 the basis
40 the majority / a minority

LESSON 2:

41 with the exception of
42 distinguish
43 the absence
44 consist of
45 confirm
46 detect
47 undoubtedly
48 permanent
49 predict
50 eventually
51 plausible
52 worthwhile
53 immensely
54 occur
55 observe
56 the objective
57 an innovation
58 interchangeable
59 attach to
60 consistent
61 a realisation
62 tremendous
63 involve
64 eliminate
65 minimal
66 exceed
67 simultaneously
68 perish
69 familiar with
70 as opposed to
71 persist in
72 return
73 competent at
74 reserve
75 stimulate
76 innate
77 reject
78 nevertheless
79 adopt
80 overly

LESSON 3:

81 confront
82 fundamental to
83 encounter
84 widespread
85 reflect
86 historical
87 available
88 ephemeral
89 the practice
90 a trend
91 typically
92 a characteristic
93 conventional
94 retain
95 harsh
96 assure that
97 mismanage
98 overburden with
99 unprecedented
100 with a view to
101 have the effect of
102 minimise
103 lead to
104 create
105 investigate into
106 surprisingly
107 perhaps
108 involved in
109 far from ...-ing
110 rely on
111 admittedly
112 make a contribution to
113 distribute
114 a tradition
115 point out that
116 solely
117 complex
118 in addition to
119 the criterion
120 outnumber

LEXICON

LESSON 4:

121 current
122 conceive that
123 acknowledge
124 numerous
125 develop
126 alleviate
127 contemporary
128 identify
129 reveal
130 convert to/into
131 (in)surmountable
132 elaborate on
133 play a role in
134 severe
135 indeed
136 invaluable
137 present at/in
138 flourish
139 evident that
140 expose to
141 -related
142 the behaviour
143 undertake
144 on the contrary
145 viable
146 the attitude
147 the alternative
148 acquire
149 the approach
150 reportedly
151 utilise
152 compound
153 have the potential to
154 have the capacity to
155 relevant to
156 readily
157 broaden
158 irrespective of
159 attempt to
160 argue that

LESSON 5:

161 (in)adequate
162 consult
163 continuously
164 speculate that
165 an occasion
166 counterbalance
167 constitute
168 prohibit
169 of concern to
170 obtain
171 vulnerable
172 extremely
173 the process
174 highlight
175 endeavour to
176 ascertain
177 not necessarily
178 tolerate
79 repeatedly
180 counter
181 comprehend
182 inundated with
183 means of
184 exceptional
185 devastate
186 adept at
187 disastrous
188 resultant
189 the priority
190 bound to
191 take measures to
192 assist
193 conflicting
194 comprise
195 then
196 dispose of
197 including
198 legislate
199 estimate that
200 debate

LESSON 6:

201 inform
202 a philosophy
203 originate from
204 evolve from
205 simplify
206 stagnate
207 pursue
208 vanish
209 adjust to
210 correct
211 defined as
212 focus on
213 unique
214 in practice
215 amount to
216 confined to
217 the transition
218 unacceptable
219 rarely
220 emphasis on
221 short-term / long-term
222 precisely
223 advocate
224 unless
225 to... , is to...
226 though
227 as... , so...
228 nor...
229 whether
230 suspect
231 destined to
232 dismiss as
233 in retrospect
234 instruct on
235 boost
236 soar
237 the phenomenon
238 the culprit
239 pivotal to
240 overall

LEXICON continued...

LESSON 7:

241 as a result of
242 catastrophic
243 complete
244 sophisticated
245 the cause
246 interact with
247 urge
248 concede
249 responsible for
250 opposed to
251 have an adverse effect on
252 a breakthrough
253 regard as
254 inquire into
255 seldom
256 initiate
257 misjudge
258 attend to
259 impending
260 deficient
261 pose
262 shortcomings
263 intermittent
264 humanity
265 deliver
266 random
267 secondary
268 date back to
269 discover
270 succumb to
271 impress
272 anti- / pro-
273 some
274 a series
275 calculate
276 (un)realistic
277 merely
278 on the premise that
279 approximately
280 criticise

LESSON 8:

281 exemplify
282 endanger
283 as well as
24 explore
285 such
286 emerge
287 detract from
288 amongst
289 with ...-ing
290 the extent
291 radically
292 further
293 mean
294 versatile
295 an obstacle
296 equipped with/for/to
297 a façade
298 an incentive
299 confident
300 naïve
301 as is the case with
302 mistaken for
303 at risk of
304 vary
305 unlike
306 temporarily
307 neglect
308 automatically
309 external / internal
310 beneficial
311 exempt from
312 a demand
313 actual
314 anticipate
315 simply
316 the (more)... , the more...
317 display
318 (un)willing to
319 aggravate
320 whereas

LESSON 9:

321 reward with
322 jeopardize
323 implement
324 in response to
325 struggle to
326 in isolation
327 restore
328 barely
329 ambitious
330 fulfil
331 welcome
332 the expertise
333 comply with
334 a section
335 conscious of
336 sufficient
337 curious
338 encompass
339 under-
340 inferior/superior to
341 sustainable
342 fail to
343 an option
344 the domain
345 perfect
346 set parameters
347 anxious to
348 the ingredients
349 ingest
350 accumulate
351 progressively
352 form
353 apparent
354 (dis)proportionately
355 prepared to
356 deem
357 prove to be
358 avert
359 hazardous to
360 -fold

LEXICON

LESSON 10:

361 address
362 a strategy
363 obsolete
364 on the verge of
365 a shortage
366 transformed
367 secure
368 reinforce
369 range from... to...
370 devise
371 assemble
372 on average
373 inconsequential
374 divide
375 locally
376 preferably
377 arise
378 voluntarily
379 tend to
380 scarce
381 adhere to
382 undermine
383 take the precaution of
384 (un)satisfactory
385 disruptive
386 an obligation
387 omit
388 remote
389 obsessed with
390 discriminate against
391 negotiate with
392 the status
393 a feature
394 eject
395 an era
396 eligible to
397 assert
398 an opponent
399 apt to
400 invade

LESSON 11:

401 a(n) (im)balance
402 thrive
403 by contrast
404 refrain from
405 discount
406 an aspiration
407 intervene
408 hamper
409 inadvertently
410 condone
411 despondent about
412 deplore
413 a deterrent
414 hypocritical
415 materialism
416 proliferate
417 prudent
418 elated
419 exhaust
420 superficial
421 resemble
422 squander
423 formerly
424 in proximity to
425 indifferent about
426 surpass
427 facilitate
428 lethargic
429 lenient
430 occupy
431 perpetuate
432 on the horizon
433 the threshold
434 prevalent
435 a combination
436 a myth
437 resume
38 dictate
439 resign
440 rectify

LESSON 12:

441 categorised as
442 preserve
443 reluctant to
444 sever
445 thorough in
446 exhibit
447 deteriorate
448 distort
449 gradually
450 existing
451 upgrade
452 select
453 irrational
454 halt
455 contemplate
456 brief
457 advance
458 namely
459 seek
460 resort to
461 compensate for
462 a remedy
463 astonishing
464 for the sake of
465 an upheaval
466 liberate
467 harness
468 tangible
469 subsequent
470 incredible
471 unthinkable
472 halve / double / treble / quadruple
473 fortify
474 precious
475 beyond
476 trivial
477 discernible
478 afterwards / beforehand
479 resent
480 urgent

LEXICON continued...

LESSON 13:

481 foresee
482 overwhelm
483 in the wake of
484 state-of-the-art
485 chaos
486 a dilemma
487 absolutely
488 extraordinary
489 delight
490 exclusive
491 thus
492 mention
493 unexpectedly
494 furthermore
495 remarkable
496 evaporate
497 irreparable
498 somewhat
499 vie for
500 (in)capable of
501 altogether
502 alarm
503 modify
504 on the condition that
505 visible
506 oblivious to
507 resist
508 succeed in/at
509 receive
510 surrender
511 sympathise with
512 abundant
513 epidemic
514 inquisitive
515 accordingly
516 authorise
517 routine
518 envisage that
519 mindful of
520 dire

LESSON 14:

521 intend to
522 genuine
523 interfere with/in
524 substitute for
525 an issue
526 compulsory
527 surround
528 subjected to
529 monitor
530 drastic
531 object to
532 on the part of
533 challenge
534 the climate
535 microscopic
536 ideal
537 hostile
538 susceptible to
539 examine
540 query
541 modest
542 the recipient
543 take heed of
544 employ
545 condemn
546 pointless
547 supposed to
548 divert
549 a decade
550 discard
551 statistically
552 (in)finite
553 (in)compatible with
554 respectively
555 understandable
556 (im)mature
557 increasingly
558 have implications for
559 in agony
560 a rapport

LESSON 15:

561 and vice versa
562 marked
563 apparently
564 contented
565 purchase
566 reside with
567 detrimental
568 satisfied
569 on a... scale
570 divorce
571 convinced that
572 suppress
573 a fluctuation
574 erratic
575 a discrepancy
576 minute
577 loathe
578 locate
579 disintegrate
580 accompany
581 in effect
582 prolong
583 (in)dispensable
584 shelter
585 intact
586 have commitments
587 channel
588 fear
589 cease
590 govern
591 elite
592 uniform
593 emphasise
594 cope with
595 by no means
596 grant
597 enjoy
598 immediately
599 (un)wise
600 prominent

LEXICON

LESSON 16:

601 suffer
602 graphic
603 gather
604 promote
605 volatile
606 a fraction
607 for the duration of
608 neutral
609 partially
610 appreciate
611 likewise
612 marginal
613 deprive of
614 logically
615 decline
616 hastily
617 suspend
618 revive
619 extract
620 verify
621 wary of
622 conspicuous
623 disillusioned with
624 blessed with
625 repulsive
626 imminent
627 upset
628 ill-
629 conversely
630 fund
631 lecture
632 shun
633 a privilege
634 primitive
635 instinctively
636 a disparity
637 obscene
638 sheer
639 lethal
640 the status quo

LESSON 17:

641 inhale
642 a phase
643 lucrative
644 materialise
645 mutual
646 coordinate
647 determined to
648 approve of
649 commonplace
650 non-existent
651 embrace
652 surface
653 eventuate
654 albeit
655 an influx
656 solitary
657 prosperous
658 dread
659 flawed
660 the introduction
661 individual
662 fiercely
663 subjective
664 (in)effective
665 conditioned to
666 minor / major
667 erroneously
668 precede
669 excel at
670 reciprocate
671 manipulate
672 relay
673 have (a) command of
674 polarise
675 abandon
676 the ratio
677 infer
678 a hierarchy
679 ongoing
680 participate in

LESSON 18:

681 the core
682 enforce
683 distinct
684 differentiate between
685 deduce
686 terminate
687 arbitrary
688 preliminary
689 progress
690 be offset by
691 equate with
692 displace
693 rigid
694 straightforward
695 concurrent
696 a bias
697 labelled as
698 a motive
699 so-called
700 adjacent to
701 adapt to
702 insert
703 orientate to/towards
704 recover
705 passive
706 scope
707 have insights into
708 communicate
709 an entity
710 flexible
711 inhibit
712 inspect
713 an agenda
714 integral
715 a sequence
716 deviate from
717 revise
718 misinformation
719 articulate
720 an interval

LEXICON continued...

LESSON 19:

721 negate
722 liberal
723 the revenue
724 supplement with
725 undergo
726 a vehicle
727 trigger
728 overlap
729 refine
730 a version
731 the volume
732 indulge in
733 reminiscent of
734 burgeoning
735 an array
736 prior
737 a mode
738 extensive
739 alienate
740 desolate
741 a notion
742 thrilling
743 potent
744 tempted to
745 overtake
746 innocent
747 incremental
748 qualify for
749 hesitate
750 exponential
751 alongside
752 venture to
753 in the interim
754 downplay
755 advisable to
756 virtually
757 notify
758 function
759 the gender
760 confuse with

LESSON 20:

761 dismantle
762 support
763 the guidance
764 experience
765 ridicule
766 presumably
767 frustrate
768 testify
769 glimpse
770 erode
771 construct
772 legally
773 subservient to
774 whereby
775 inflict on
776 deliberately
777 deposit
778 outspoken
779 vacant
780 travel
781 the magnitude
782 deceptive
783 underestimate
784 take for granted
785 immune
786 promising
787 worship
788 reason that
789 an ultimatum
790 bewilder
791 from the outset
792 cooperate with
793 fare well
794 enthusiastic about
795 remain
796 dispense with
797 significant
798 a mission
799 insofar as
800 at the expense of

LESSON 21:

801 notorious
802 attract
803 mainstream
804 envious of
805 a contradiction
806 ruthless
807 engulf
808 the stamina
809 accountable to/for
810 (un)wittingly
811 on the brink of
812 (un)intelligible
813 coerce into
814 antiquated
815 contrary to
816 complacent
817 fatal
818 (un)warranted
819 accelerate
820 dominate
821 propose
822 ponder
823 diminish
824 along with
825 commercially
826 signal
827 a boom
828 (in)edible
829 yet
830 versus
831 an opportunity
832 appeal to
833 dramatic
834 isolate
835 even so
836 request
837 declare
838 strengthen
839 grounds for
840 expand

LEXICON

LESSON 22:

841 coincide with
842 an escalation
843 strike
844 confiscate
845 relieve
846 discourage
847 vast
848 recognize
849 perceive as
850 offer
851 unavoidable
852 desire
853 extreme
854 counterproductive
855 lessen
856 affluent
857 remaining
858 associated with
859 quantify
860 hence
861 evaluate
862 protest
863 much of
864 collaborate
865 cover
866 document
867 elsewhere
868 on the point of
869 irrevocable
870 alter
871 comparable
872 entail
873 convey
874 devote
875 depict as
876 deplete
877 maximum
878 keep pace with
879 sizeable
880 gauge

LESSON 23:

881 otherwise
882 a degree
883 a period
884 the former / the latter
885 the nature
886 leaving aside
887 daily
888 compete with/for
889 preventable
890 subscribe to
891 a component
892 represent
893 optimistic
894 emulate
895 sacrifice
896 differ
897 rapid
898 thereby
899 remove
900 invite
901 indicate
902 rather than
903 generate
904 determine
905 exclude
906 underlying
907 the infrastructure
908 appropriate
909 realise
910 justify
911 rank
912 essential
913 consequently
914 be largely due to
915 to the extent that
916 the factors
917 a misconception
918 inherit
919 belong to
920 periodically

LESSON 24:

921 assume
922 specifically
923 the existence
924 controversial
925 sceptical
926 have an impact on
927 a diversity
928 in part
929 establish
930 compelling
931 ultimately
932 enhance
933 lie in/with
934 derive from
935 enable to
936 surely
937 basically
938 provide with
939 provided that
940 relatively
941 take into account
942 regardless of
943 claim
944 initially
945 survive
946 a certain number/ amount
947 at least
948 a prospect
949 (dis)advantage
950 exacerbate
951 accomplish
952 restrict
953 given that
954 a contributor
955 the outcome
956 concentrate on/in
957 —ly, -wise
958 previously
959 {other time phrases}
960 invariably

LEXICON continued...

LESSON 25:

961 exploit
962 universal
963 have access to
964 far outweigh
965 the equivalent
966 demonstrate
967 suggest
968 critical of
969 according to
970 (ir)rational
971 an aspect
972 appear
973 (in)directly related to
974 benefit from
975 obviously
976 extend
977 ensure
978 feasible
979 the sector
980 noticeable
981 devoid of
982 imply
983 inevitable
984 respond to
985 questionable
986 proceed
987 clearly
988 frequently
989 assess
990 reach the stage
991 considerably
992 theoretically
993 possess
994 primarily
995 entire
996 predominantly
997 have a perception
998 maintain
999 negligible
1000 release
1001 aware of/that

*"Did you learn at least five words today?
The best work is a little work each day."*

Keith Burgess

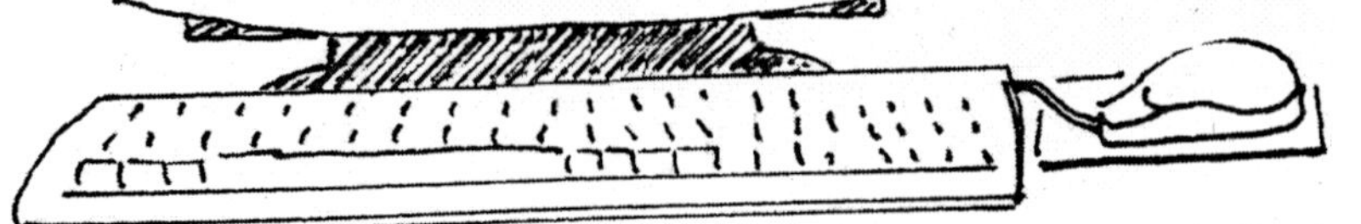